SAINSBURY'S
VEGETARIAN COOKERY
VOLUME TWO

SARAH BROWN

SAINSBURY'S
VEGETARIAN COOKERY
VOLUME TWO
SARAH BROWN

■ CONTENTS ■

CONTRIBUTING AUTHORS

Ian Burleigh

Roselyne Masselin

Christine Smith

Published exclusively for J Sainsbury plc,
Stamford House, Stamford Street, London SE1 9LL by
Dorling Kindersley Limited, 9 Henrietta Street,
London WC2E 8PS

First published 1990

Copyright © 1990 by Dorling Kindersley Limited,
London

Text copyright © 1990 by
Sarah Elizabeth Brown Limited

ISBN 0 86318 440 5

Printed and bound in Italy by Graphicom

*H*ere are some 200 of my favourite recipes to give plenty of imaginative ideas and tasty results when you are looking for an alternative to meat and fish.

There are soups and starters that make delicious appetisers for any meal or light snacks in their own right. As for main courses, I've suggested many different possibilities. Classic dishes such as casseroles and quiches are always popular, and I've included ideas that may introduce you to new and different combinations of ingredients that will extend your own culinary repertoire. To finish there are some tempting puddings, as well as refreshing fruit desserts.

Many of the recipes in this book are simple and quick to make, just the thing for family suppers and mid-week meals. Apart from everyday fare, you'll find lots of ideas that are suitable for entertaining. There are elegant centrepieces for dinner parties, and delicious light savouries for buffets. Often the preparation for these meals can be done well ahead of time, leaving the minimum of work to do at the last minute.

As well as providing you with many interesting recipes that make a change from meat and fish, this book shows you how to make the most of wholesome unrefined foods. These ingredients, such as brown rice, beans, wholemeal flour and wholewheat pasta, are all high in fibre and low in fats, an ideal combination that is so important in developing a modern healthy diet.

Another advantage of wholefoods is their long shelf life. Packets and cans of beans, rice and pasta are all useful to have in your store-cupboard, making it easier to plan meals and to cope with unexpected guests.

Fresh foods such as fruit and vegetables are important for your health too. The recipes here use a wide range of fresh produce, which provide you with essential vitamins and minerals, as well as being a colourful and flavoursome addition to any dish. There are ideas for all year round to help you make the most of seasonal foods, and save money too. A light vegetable soup served chilled for example is ideal for warm summer days. Add to that a good variety of salads, and fresh fruit desserts and you've got an attractive feast. Serve hearty broths, chunky casseroles and old-fashioned puddings as cheering food in colder weather.

You'll find something here which will appeal to all the family on many different occasions. If you are already vegetarian and looking for inspiration, or if you simply fancy a change from meat and fish, I hope you will be tempted to try lots of the ideas in this book, and I'm quite sure you'll enjoy eating the results.

Sarah Brown

POD, LEAF AND SHOOT VEGETABLES

*T*hese vegetables are excellent sources of vitamins, minerals and fibre. Buy them very fresh, store in a cool, dark place and use as soon as possible.

GREEN BEANS

Green beans are a member of the large runner bean family and need topping and tailing before cooking.

MANGETOUT

A variety of pea with an edible pod, mangetout are a rich source of fibre. A good side vegetable, they also combine well with rice.

OKRA

Okra are available fresh, canned and dried and can be eaten raw or cooked. Use as a vegetable or as a thickener for stews and soups.

SWEETCORN

Corn on the cob is available fresh or frozen. Buy the kernels off the husk, canned or frozen. Baby sweetcorn cobs can also be found.

SPINACH

An excellent source of folic acid, calcium and iron, spinach is delicious with eggs or in soups, bakes and salads.

FRISÉE
(curly endive)

Frisée has a slightly sharp flavour and makes an attractive salad base.

COS LETTUCE

Cos or round lettuce is available all year. It has a sharp flavour and coarse, elongated leaves.

ROUND LETTUCE

This standard lettuce should have a large, firm heart and loose, unblemished leaves. It is available all year round.

ICEBERG LETTUCE

Iceberg is far more densely packed than other lettuces. It is crisp and sweet and usually pale in colour.

CHINESE LEAVES

Chinese leaves have a light, crunchy texture and can be eaten raw in salads or cooked in soups, and stir fries.

RED CABBAGE

Red cabbage is deliciously crunchy and, since it keeps for a long time, is easy to store.

CAULIFLOWER

Cauliflower is a member of the cabbage family, available all year round.

WATERCRESS

This nutritious leaf with its clean peppery taste is excellent in stir-fries, soups, salads and as a garnish.

CHICORY

Chicory is slightly bitter in taste. Choose the whitest and eat raw or cooked.

BRUSSELS SPROUTS

These winter "miniature cabbages" originated near Brussels in the Middle Ages. They are rich in folic acid and taste best when small and young.

FENNEL

Sliced fennel has a taste of aniseed and looks much like celery. Eat raw or cooked.

CELERY

Celery can be bought all year round and is sold fresh and canned. Store celery in an airtight container in the fridge, but use as quickly as possible.

BROCCOLI

Broccoli is a variety of cauliflower. It is rich in Vitamins A and C, makes an excellent side dish and combines well with nuts in light casseroles.

SPRING ONIONS

Also known as scallions, these young onions are eaten in stir-fries and salads.

CRESS

Usually eaten with mustard. This sprout contains essential vitamins and minerals.

LEEKS

Leeks are milder than onions and suitable for soups and stews. Leeks can also be served as a main vegetable.

RED (Spanish) and PICKLING ONIONS

Pickling onions are picked when the bulb has just formed. Red onions are mild and sweet.

BEAN SPROUTS

Mung bean sprouts are grown commercially in ideal conditions. They should be eaten on the day of purchase and rinsed before use.

RADICCHIO

This Italian red chicory has a slightly bitter flavour and is a colourful addition to salads.

ASPARAGUS

The young shoots are available fresh in spring and early summer and canned for use throughout the year.

7

ROOT AND FRUIT
■ VEGETABLES ■

*R*oots should be scrubbed, not peeled, to preserve the nutrients that are just under the skin. Fruit vegetables, used very fresh, add colour and texture to a dish.

BEETROOT

Beetroot is a very versatile root vegetable, available all year round.

CELERIAC

This vegetable looks like turnip but tastes like celery. It must be peeled before eating.

TURNIP

Turnip is available all year round. Delicious in stews and soups.

MOOLI

Also known as daikon and winter radish, this white Japanese radish is milder and has more nutritional value than red spring ones.

KOHL RABI

Kohl rabi is a type of cabbage and can be purple or green. Cook like turnip.

SWEET POTATO

Sweet potato, a variety of which is known as yam, is a sweet, root vegetable. Use in the same way as ordinary potato.

RADISHES

Early spring radishes have a less peppery flavour than later crops. Store in iced water in the fridge for a crisp texture.

PARSNIP

A winter root vegetable. The sweetish taste makes it suitable for curries, purées and glazed desserts.

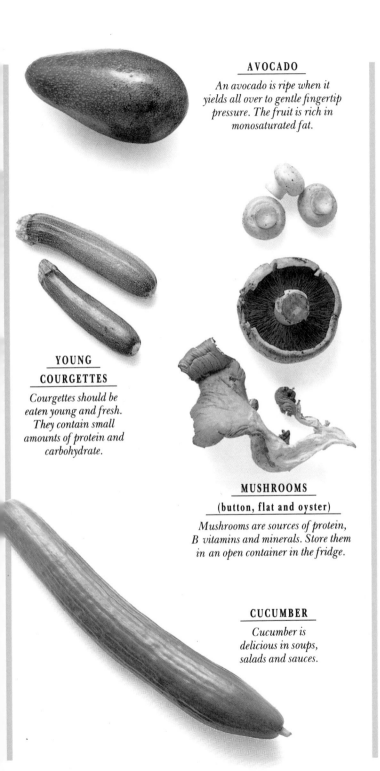
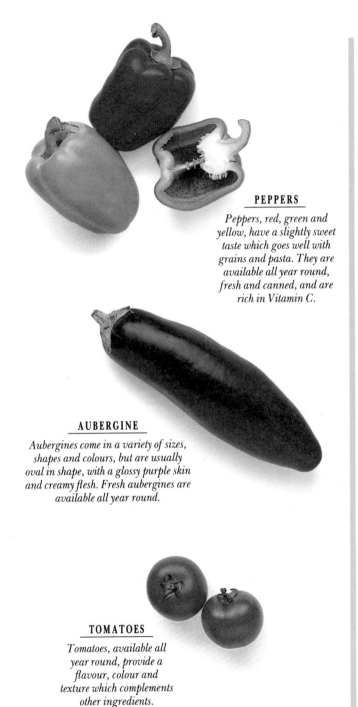

AVOCADO

An avocado is ripe when it yields all over to gentle fingertip pressure. The fruit is rich in monosaturated fat.

PEPPERS

Peppers, red, green and yellow, have a slightly sweet taste which goes well with grains and pasta. They are available all year round, fresh and canned, and are rich in Vitamin C.

YOUNG
COURGETTES

Courgettes should be eaten young and fresh. They contain small amounts of protein and carbohydrate.

AUBERGINE

Aubergines come in a variety of sizes, shapes and colours, but are usually oval in shape, with a glossy purple skin and creamy flesh. Fresh aubergines are available all year round.

MUSHROOMS
(button, flat and oyster)

Mushrooms are sources of protein, B vitamins and minerals. Store them in an open container in the fridge.

CUCUMBER

Cucumber is delicious in soups, salads and sauces.

TOMATOES

Tomatoes, available all year round, provide a flavour, colour and texture which complements other ingredients.

FLOURS AND PULSES

*T*hese thicken and give substance to a dish. Pulses are available dried and canned. If dried, all except split peas and lentils must be soaked and boiled vigorously to destroy natural toxins.

WHOLEMEAL FLOUR

A high-gluten flour, extensively used in all kinds of baking, and recently to make pasta. It can be combined with other flours for variety and is a good source of fibre, E and B Vitamins. The Vitamin E goes rancid eventually, so use within 2–3 months.

STRONG WHITE/
UNBLEACHED
WHITE FLOUR

A "strong" flour is a high-gluten flour containing 10–14 per cent wheat protein, or gluten. White flour is made from the endosperm (what is left when the husk and germ are removed). It contains iron, calcium and Vitamin B_1.

BUCKWHEAT FLOUR

Buckwheat is not a cereal, but a plant related to rhubarb and sorrel, which can be ground to a meal and used in baking. Its seeds are also available and can be roasted before use. Buckwheat is rich in protein.

BUTTER BEANS

Used in soups, bakes, casseroles and salads, these have a sweeter relative, the lima bean. They are also excellent puréed in stuffings and sauces.

HARICOT BEANS

These are good, tender beans to purée for sauces and casseroles. They are the popular "baked beans" canned in tomato sauce.

RED KIDNEY BEANS

Red kidney beans are pleasantly sweet and range from dark pink to maroon in colour.

MUNG BEANS

Mung beans are popular for sprouting because of their sweet taste and high vitamin content, which when sprouted can increase by 600 per cent, especially Vitamin B.

BLACK EYE BEANS

A tender bean that absorbs other flavours well; ideal for bakes, soups and casseroles.

BLACK KIDNEY
BEANS

Particularly popular throughout Spain and Central and South America, their sweet taste is delicious in soups and casseroles, especially with cumin, bay leaf, tomatoes and garlic.

FLAGEOLET BEANS

A popular ingredient in Italian cuisine, with a delicate, subtle taste.

GREEN SPLIT PEAS

Delicious in soups, especially with some fresh mint. Split peas do not require soaking.

YELLOW SPLIT PEAS

These are sweeter than whole peas, and ideal as a base for soups. They do not require soaking.

CHICK PEAS

These crunchy, nutty beans are rich in minerals. Best known in hummus, they are good in many dishes, and are easily sprouted.

CONTINENTAL LENTILS
(green lentils)

Like the smaller red lentils, continental or green lentils do not require soaking, but they do not cook to a pulp. They are important in many Indian dishes.

RED SPLIT LENTILS

Especially rich in fibre, these small lentils do not need soaking and cook to a pulp. They are an important part of many Middle Eastern dishes.

LASAGNE

Flat strips of pasta suitable for baked dishes, there are several kinds of lasagne available, including a "no pre-cook" variety.

TAGLIATELLE

This ribbon pasta can be bought fresh or dried, and also flavoured with spinach as tagliatelle verde.

CANNELLONI

These are large hollow tubes of pasta which, like lasagne, are used for baked dishes, stuffed and with a sauce.

■ NUTS, GRAINS AND SEEDS ■

vailable whole, flaked, nibbed or milled, these are all rich in protein, vitamins and unrefined carbohydrates. They should be kept in cool, dry, airtight conditions.

WALNUTS

Ripe brown walnuts are a rich source of protein and unsaturated fat. Green, unripe Vitamin C-rich walnuts are usually pickled.

WHOLE ALMONDS   ALMOND FLAKES

GROUND ALMONDS

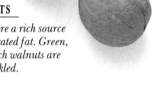

CASHEWS

Although usually sold shelled and salted, healthier, unsalted cashews are available.

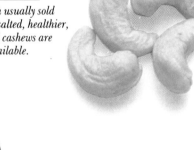

BRAZIL NUTS

High in protein, Brazils are usually sold whole and shelled.

ALMONDS

High in protein, almonds can be used whole or flaked as a garnish or in salads, sauces and stuffings, or ground to replace some of the flour in a recipe.

PECAN NUTS

A relative of the walnut, this nut is rich in vitamins and minerals. Stand in boiling water for 15–20 minutes before shelling.

PEANUTS

Strictly speaking a legume, since they grow in a pod rather than in a shell, peanuts are very high in B and E vitamins.

SWEET (or Spanish)
CHESTNUTS

Good puréed, these nuts are rich in B and E Vitamins and low in fat.

HAZELNUTS

A good culinary nut, with high protein levels. Use in salads, loaves or rissoles.

FRESH COCONUT

The coconut is valuable for both its sweet flesh and its milk, and is used in much Indian cookery, rice dishes and desserts.

SHORT-GRAIN
BROWN RICE

Unprocessed rice containing valuable nutrients, this has a nutty texture and flavour.

PORRIDGE OATS

These are made from groats (hulled grains) broken by rolling. Oats are high in protein, iron and B Vitamins.

PINE KERNELS

The seeds of the Mediterranean stone pine, known as pignoli, are sold shelled, roasted and sometimes salted.

SEMOLINA

Semolina is made from particles of hard durum wheat.

SUNFLOWER SEEDS

Rich in polyunsaturates, proteins, vitamins and minerals, sunflower seeds can be eaten raw or roasted, or used in bakes.

HERBS AND SPICES

*H*erbs and spices are essential to the nature of any dish. Herbs are best used fresh – if bought dried they must be stored in airtight containers. Buy spices whole and grate or grind them as you need them.

BAY LEAVES

Used as a leaf or in bouquet garni to flavour casseroles. Bay leaves must be removed before serving.

BASIL

Fresh basil is a very versatile herb which combines well with garlic in soups and sauces.

CHERVIL

Chervil has a delicate flavour which is diminished by cooking, so add it just before serving.

MARJORAM

Sometimes included in bouquet garni, this herb keeps its flavour well when dried.

SAGE

A strongly-flavoured herb, sage can be used to counter over-rich foods. Combines well with pea- and bean-based soups.

THYME

Thyme is a popular herb, containing an oil which aids the digestion of fatty foods. It mixes well with other herbs.

MINT

Mint has a clean, fresh taste which complements light soups, fruit-based starters, simple mousses, sorbets and leafy salad vegetables.

OREGANO

The wild form of marjoram, oregano is widely used in Italian cookery.

ROSEMARY
(fresh and dried)

Dries well and complements beans and vegetables.

PARSLEY

Both curled (above) and flat parsley are rich in iron and Vitamin C. Dried parsley is available, but has less flavour than fresh.

DILL SEEDS

Dill seeds taste rather like caraway and go well in garnishes, sauces and pickles.

DILL

Fresh dill, or dill weed, combines well with vegetable soups and salads.

GINGER

Root ginger can be bought whole, dried or ground.

CINNAMON

Use cinnamon in sweet soups and starters.

GARLIC

Usually associated with Mediterranean and Eastern cookery. Garlic is thought to have properties which help "thin" the blood and prevent clots.

GARAM MASALA

This blend of cinnamon, cloves, cumin and mace can be bought ready-mixed and is important in Indian cookery.

ALLSPICE

These dried berries taste of cloves, cinnamon and nutmeg.

CHIVES

Related to the onion but subtler in taste, less sulphurous and easier to digest. They should be fresh or freeze-dried.

BLACK
PEPPERCORNS

Black peppercorns can be ground or used whole.

CARDAMOM
PODS

The green pods from a ginger-related plant contain dark, spicy seeds.

BOUQUET GARNI

Bouquet garni – mixed dried herbs wrapped in muslin or a sachet – adds a rich flavour.

PAPRIKA

Made from ground pimiento seeds, it ranges from mildly hot to sweet.

NUTMEG
and MACE

Native to Indonesia, nutmeg is a sweet dried nut: mace is its savoury husk.

CARAWAY SEEDS

A strong, pungent spice, extensively used in Europe in many savoury dishes as well as bread and cheese making.

CUMIN

A flavouring much used in Eastern dishes, available crushed and as whole seeds. The seeds are more pungent.

CHILLI POWDER

CHILLI PEPPERS

All chilli is hot, including the more commonly used powder.

CAPERS

The pickled flower buds of a Mediterranean shrub.

FRESH CHILLI

15

FLAVOURINGS AND ■ DAIRY PRODUCTS ■

*D*airy products are good sources of protein and calcium, and there are now many low-fat alternatives available. There is also a wide range of healthy flavourings that may be used instead of sugar and salt.

YOGURT

Made from whole or skimmed milk and left to ferment under controlled conditions by the action of bacteria. Greek yogurt is more concentrated.

COTTAGE CHEESE

Made from cooked, skimmed cow's milk that is drained and coated with thin cream. Rich in protein, Vitamins B_2 and B_{12} and calcium.

HORSERADISH

Grated horseradish can be used with sour cream to create a spicy sauce.

PEANUT BUTTER

An excellent, healthy ingredient for dips, sauces and dressings.

TOMATO PURÉE

A purée made from tomato concentrate, and indispensable on pizzas and in most pasta dishes.

DIJON MUSTARD

Dijon mustard is hot, ideal for adding spice to mild soups or giving a light dressing extra tang.

CURD CHEESE

This medium-fat soft cheese is made from the separated curds of whole milk set without rennet.

CHEDDAR

Cheddars come in a variety of colours, and maturity. There are low-fat and vegetarian (animal rennet-free) varieties.

TABASCO

Tabasco is a hot relish which lends a spicy flavour to Mexican-style dishes.

PARMESAN CHEESE

*Made from curds, heated,
salted and pressed.*

SKIMMED MILK SOFT CHEESE

(quark)

*Quark is a low-fat, protein-rich, soft
cheese made from skimmed milk. It has a
mild flavour and creamy texture which
makes it a versatile ingredient in any
recipe. Use as a healthier alternative to
cream cheese.*

RICOTTA

*Ricotta is a mild, unripened Italian
cheese with a light, creamy taste, which
is made from the whey of cow's, sheep's
or goat's milk.*

SMETANA

*Made from skimmed milk and cream,
this low-fat alternative to cream is
delicious in desserts or stirred
into soups.*

SOYA SAUCE

*A thin, salty sauce made from
fermented soya beans, this is one of
the main flavourings in
Chinese cookery.*

CHÈVRE

(goat's cheese)

*Mild but tangy, with a good
mineral balance.*

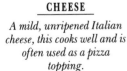

MOZZARELLA

CHEESE

*A mild, unripened Italian
cheese, this cooks well and is
often used as a pizza
topping.*

FIRM TOFU

*A hard-pressed soya bean curd,
high in protein, low in fat, and
rich in lecithin – a fat that helps
regulate cholesterol levels
in the body.*

TREE FRUIT (CITRUS AND TROPICAL)

*C*itrus fruit and an increasing range of tropical fruit are now available year round. Citrus fruit keep a long time in a cool place: tropical fruit are best bought under-ripe and allowed to ripen at home.

RED DESSERT APPLE

The North American Empire has a sweet flavour and an attractive colour for fruit salads and other desserts. The Spartan and the Starking are also good red eating apples with a sweet flavour.

LIME

Slightly sweeter and more delicate than lemons, sweet limes make a refreshing flavouring. The freshest limes have dark, shiny, tight skins.

GREEN DESSERT APPLE

The Granny Smith, originally from Australia, has a distinctively sharp, crisp flavour and a good colour. It is available all year round.

WILLIAM PEAR

A good late summer dessert pear, the William is best bought when firm and eaten as soon as it is ripe.

ORANGES

There are several types of sweet orange, eaten in desserts, and bitter oranges, used in cooking and marmalade. All are rich in Vitamin C.

LEMON

Lemon rind and juice is invaluable for garnishing and flavouring sweet and savoury dishes.

GREENGAGE

This sweet variety of dessert plum turns amber when fully ripe, and is in season only in the early autumn.

PACKHAM PEAR

Crisper and sharper than the William, the Packham is excellent raw or cooked and is in season from May to August.

PINK GRAPEFRUIT

Grapefruit are high in Vitamin C. The pink variety are often juicier than the white and are sweet enough to eat without added sugar.

DESSERT PLUM

Best eaten soon after they are ripe, dessert plums, such as Victorias (above) should have a firm, unblemished skin.

COOKING PLUM

Available all year round, except in early spring, plums should be cooked when ripe for the sweetest flavour.

BANANA

Bananas are rich in fibre. Delicious raw, baked or flambéed, they are best bought when yellow with just a tinge of brown.

PINEAPPLE

When ripe, fresh pineapples have a sweet smell and easily detached leaves. Eat within a few days of ripening. Choose canned pineapple in natural juice as an alternative.

MANGO

Delicious fresh for desserts, this Indian fruit is also made into chutneys. It is available in cans.

APRICOT

There are two crops, summer and mid- to late-winter. When eating raw, choose ripe, dark-coloured fruit for a sweet flavour. Canned apricots are known to retain a good flavour.

CANTALOUPE
MELON

The charentais, (left), is a small, sweet variety of the cantaloupe. Cut pieces will keep for up to 2 days if sealed from the air.

PASSION
FRUIT

Choose the largest fruit available for the juiciest pulp.

HONEYDEW
MELON

Like other melons, the honeydew is available all year round and is ripe when the stalk end gives slightly.

PEACH

There are two types of peach – "freestone" for eating and "clingstone" for cooking. The smaller and paler fruits often have the best flavour.

KIWI FRUIT
(Chinese
gooseberry)

These delicate New Zealand fruit are rich in Vitamin C. The season is late spring to mid-summer, but they freeze well for up to 6 months.

NECTARINE

A cross between a peach and a plum, the smooth-skinned nectarine should be eaten when pink and slightly soft.

WATERMELON

The watermelon, a different genus from other melons, contains 91 per cent water. Serve it cold for a refreshing, low-calorie dessert.

BERRIES, VINES AND ■ DRIED FRUIT ■

*A*ll these fruits are high in fibre; dried fruit is the highest. Buy soft fruit in season and slightly under-ripe, and handle carefully to avoid bruising. Dried fruit keeps up to a year in an airtight container.

BLACKCURRANTS

Rich in Vitamin C and iron, blackcurrants make an excellent dessert fruit and are always eaten cooked.

RASPBERRIES

Red, white and black raspberries are all rich in iron and freeze more successfully than strawberries. Avoid punnets with stains at the base.

REDCURRANTS

Slightly sweeter than other currants, but equally rich in Vitamin C, the red variety can be eaten raw when ripe.

BLACKBERRIES

Found either cultivated or wild in the hedgerows in the autumn, blackberries are a good source of fibre. When picking your own for cooking, include some red berries for a piquant flavour.

BLACK CHERRIES

There are two species of cherry; sweet, eating cherries with either red or black skins, and bitter cherries, such as Morellos, for cooking.

CRANBERRIES

These winter berries, which are grown in the USA, keep and freeze well inside their protective, waxy skins.

SEEDLESS WHITE GRAPES

Available from January to June, the seedless varieties of grape are generally smaller and sweeter than seeded.

BLUEBERRIES

Like most soft fruit, blueberries are available in mid-summer. They have a tart flavour and are eaten raw or cooked with natural sweetening.

STRAWBERRIES

Since they lose flavour and texture when frozen, it is best to buy fresh strawberries, now available at most times of year.

PRUNES

These dried black plums are low in calories, but high in fibre and the tenderised variety can be cooked in 8 minutes. Prunes are sold with or without stones.

DRIED DATES

Dried dessert dates are sold unstoned, while cooking dates are sold stoned in blocks.

BLACK GRAPES

The tough skin on black grapes adds colour and fibre to desserts.

SULTANAS

These are large, sweet dried grapes, high in nutritional value.

DRIED APRICOTS

Dried apricots are extremely high in Vitamin A, protein, fibre, and iron. Try to avoid those preserved in sugar — dried apricots are naturally sweet anyway.

DRIED FIGS

Figs, an excellent source of fibre, are available fresh in summer and autumn, and dried all year. Dried figs are rich in minerals.

DRIED PEACHES

An excellent source of iron, dried peaches can be easily reconstituted by soaking in fresh water.

DESICCATED COCONUT

Dried, grated coconut, which makes an excellent flavouring, is also sold as flakes, powder or compressed into blocks known as creamed coconut.

STARTERS AND DIPS

CLOCKWISE FROM TOP LEFT: Tofu dip (see p.24); Haricot guacamole (see p.24); Blue cheese and butter bean dip (see p.24)

■ HARICOT GUACAMOLE ■

INGREDIENTS

■ 4–6oz (125–175g) haricot beans, soaked, or a 15oz (430g) can of cannelini beans, drained
■ 1 avocado, peeled, stoned and mashed
■ 2 cloves garlic, crushed
■ 4 tbsp (60ml) lemon juice
■ 4–6 tbsp (60–90ml) natural yogurt
■ salt and pepper

Illustrated on page 23

The avocado used in guacamole, a traditional Mexican dip, should be very ripe for the best flavour. Mashed beans add to the texture and flavour without spoiling the creaminess of the dip. To save time use any can of white beans, drain and follow the recipe from step 2.

PREPARATION TIME: 10 mins (plus 10–12 hours soaking time)
COOKING TIME: 40–45 mins for the beans
SERVES 4

METHOD

1 If using dried beans, drain and place in a pan with plenty of fresh water. Bring to the boil and boil fast for 10 minutes, then cover and simmer for 30–35 minutes or until soft. Drain well.
2 Mash the beans with all the remaining ingredients, either by hand or in a blender or food processor. Season to taste.
3 Serve with vegetable crudités or Melba toast.

■ BLUE CHEESE ■ AND BUTTER BEAN DIP ■

INGREDIENTS

■ 4–6 oz (125–175g) dried butter beans, soaked or a 15oz (430g) can
■ 4oz (125g) blue cheese
■ salt and pepper
■ bunch of watercress

Illustrated on page 23

Mashed beans are an excellent way of making rich dips go a good deal further, and also add to the protein and fibre content. If using canned beans, drain and follow the method from step 2.

PREPARATION TIME: 10 mins (plus 10–12 hours soaking time)
COOKING TIME: 40–50 mins for the beans
SERVES 4

METHOD

1 Drain the beans. Place in a pan with plenty of fresh water and bring to the boil. Boil fast for 10 minutes, then cover and simmer for 30–40 minutes or until soft. Drain well and cool.
2 Mash the butter beans with the cheese until completely smooth. Season to taste.
3 Serve on a bed of watercress with wholemeal bread or vegetable crudités.

■ TOFU DIP ■

INGREDIENTS

■ 10oz (300g) silken tofu (bean curd)
■ 1–2 cloves garlic, crushed
■ 2 tbsp (30ml) lemon juice
■ 1 tbsp (15ml) sunflower oil (optional)
■ soya sauce to taste
■ salt and pepper

Illustrated on page 23

This is one of the easiest ways of using tofu (bean curd) as the base for creamy dips or cold sauces. Silken tofu will blend to the consistency of thick cream and absorb other flavours so that it can be used for both savoury and sweet recipes. Tofu is high in protein, cholesterol-free and very low in fat, making it an ideal alternative to yogurt and a healthier choice than mayonnaise.

PREPARATION TIME: 10 mins
SERVES 4

METHOD

1 Blend the tofu with the garlic, lemon and oil in a blender or food processor, until completely smooth.
2 Season to taste with soya sauce, salt and pepper. Serve with vegetable crudités.

■ AVOCADO ■ AND CORIANDER DIP ■

INGREDIENTS

■ 1 avocado, peeled and stoned
■ 2 tbsp (30ml) lemon juice
■ 5 tbsp (75ml) natural yogurt
■ 2 tbsp (30ml) finely chopped fresh coriander leaves
■ salt and pepper

GARNISH
■ slice of lemon
■ slice of lime

Illustrated right

The smooth texture of avocado and its delicate colour make it an ideal base for dips. It is rich, however, so use it sparingly.
PREPARATION TIME: 15 mins (plus 1 hour standing time)
SERVES 3–4

METHOD

1 In a blender, mix the avocado with the lemon juice and yogurt until completely smooth.
2 Stir in the coriander.
3 Season to taste, then leave the dip to stand for about an hour to allow the flavours to develop.
4 Garnish with a slice of lemon and a slice of lime and serve with crudités.

FROM TOP: *Cucumber dip with herbs (see p.26); Avocado and coriander dip; Savoury cashew cream; Hot Spanish dip*

SAVOURY CASHEW ◼ CREAM ◼

Nut dressings and creams are ideal as dips, salad dressings or as sauces for stuffed vegetables or rissoles. They are all made by adding liquid to a ground nut base and will thicken when left to stand.

PREPARATION TIME: 10 mins (plus standing time)

SERVES 6

INGREDIENTS

◼ 4 oz (125g) cashew nuts
◼ up to ⅓ pint (200ml) water
◼ 1–2 tbsp (15–30ml) finely chopped fresh herbs
◼ 1–2 tsp (5–10ml) soya sauce
◼ salt and pepper

Illustrated left

METHOD

1 In a blender or food processor, grind the cashew nuts thoroughly to a fine powder.
2 Add the water gradually, stirring continuously, to form a thick cream.
3 Add fresh herbs and soya sauce to flavour. Season to taste.
4 Leave to stand for 1–2 hours before serving.

◼ HOT SPANISH DIP ◼

The vivid colour and strong taste make this dip a welcome low-calorie addition to any salad table. The vegetables need to be chopped very finely, to produce a smooth texture.

PREPARATION TIME: 20 mins

SERVES 4

INGREDIENTS

◼ 2 tomatoes, skinned
◼ ½ green pepper, deseeded
◼ ½ red pepper, deseeded
◼ 1 green chilli, deseeded
◼ 2 tbsp (30ml) olive oil
◼ 1 tbsp (15ml) red wine
◼ 1–2 cloves garlic, crushed
◼ salt and pepper

GARNISH
◼ sprig of mint

Illustrated left

METHOD

1 Prepare all the vegetables and chop very finely or mince.
2 In a bowl, mix the olive oil, red wine and garlic, add to the vegetables and stir thoroughly.
3 Season to taste. Garnish with mint and serve with courgette crudités and black olives.

CUCUMBER DIP
■ WITH HERBS ■

INGREDIENTS

- 4oz (125g) skimmed milk soft cheese (or quark, ricotta or curd cheese)
- 6 tbsp (90ml) natural yogurt
- ¼ cucumber, peeled and finely diced
- 2 tsp (10ml) fresh chives or dill weed
- 1 tbsp (15ml) lemon juice
- salt and pepper

GARNISH

- sprig of dill or chopped chives

Illustrated on page 25

The combination of soft cheese and yogurt makes a creamy base for a dip and contributes a surprising amount of protein. The texture of the cucumber complements the refreshing watermelon and green bean crudités.

PREPARATION TIME: 10 mins (plus chilling time)

SERVES 4

METHOD

1 In a blender, mix together the soft cheese and the yogurt.
2 Add the finely diced cucumber, the herbs and lemon juice.
3 Season to taste, garnish with dill and serve chilled with chunks of watermelon and green beans.

Falafels with tahini sauce

FALAFELS
■ WITH TAHINI SAUCE ■

INGREDIENTS

- 4–6oz (125–175g) chick peas, soaked for ten to twelve hours
- 2 tbsp (30ml) lemon juice
- 2–3 tbsp (30–45ml) chopped fresh coriander
- 2–3 tbsp (30–45ml) chopped fresh parsley
- 2 cloves garlic, crushed
- 1 tsp (5ml) cumin seeds
- 1 tsp (5ml) coriander seeds
- 1 tbsp (15ml) sesame seeds
- 2–3 tsp (10–15ml) soya sauce
- salt and pepper
- sunflower oil for shallow frying

TAHINI SAUCE

- 2 tbsp (30ml) tahini
- 2–3 tbsp (30–45ml) water
- 2 tsp (10ml) soya sauce
- 2 tbsp (30ml) lemon juice
- 2–3tbsp (30–45ml) natural yogurt
- 1 clove garlic, crushed (optional)

Illustrated left

A traditional dish from the Middle East using a raw chick pea mixture flavoured with herbs and spices. The falafels are usually deep fried but can be shallow fried as long as the oil is hot enough at the start to enable the mixture to seal together instantly, and as long as the falafels are turned frequently. Tahini is a paste made from crushed sesame seeds, and is a very rich source of calcium, while chick peas, often eaten in the form of a dip called hummus, are a good source of zinc and a number of other minerals. This starter could easily be made in advance and then heated through just before serving.

PREPARATION TIME: 25 mins (plus 10–12 hours soaking time)

COOKING TIME: 5–7 mins per batch

SERVES 4

METHOD

1 Drain the chick peas well, rinse thoroughly and drain again.
2 Grind the chick peas to a powder in a food processor or grinder.
3 Add the lemon juice, fresh herbs and garlic.
4 Lightly toast the seeds in a dry frying pan, then crush using a pestle and mortar. Add to the chick pea mixture with the soya sauce.
5 Mix all the falafel ingredients together in a blender or food processor. Season well. Shape the mixture into 12 walnut-sized balls.
6 Heat the oil and fry about 4 falafels at a time until golden brown in colour, turning frequently. Drain on kitchen paper and keep warm.
7 For the sauce, gradually mix the tahini with the water, then add the remaining ingredients. This sauce will thicken on standing so you may want to add extra yogurt.

Chick pea dip

■ CRUNCHY ORANGE DIP ■

INGREDIENTS

■ 4oz (125g)
skimmed milk soft
cheese (or quark,
ricotta or curd
cheese)
■ 6 tbsp (90ml)
natural yogurt
■ rind and juice of
1 orange
■ 1oz (25g) sesame
seeds
■ 1 tsp (5ml)
coriander seeds
■ salt and pepper

Illustrated below

Sharp citrus flavours go well with a smooth
soft cheese base and make a good acid/
alkali balance. Here, roasted sesame and
coriander seeds add flavour, texture and
protein to the dip.

PREPARATION TIME: 15 mins

SERVES 4

METHOD

1 In a blender, mix together the soft
cheese, yogurt, orange rind and juice.
2 Roast the sesame and coriander seeds in
a heavy pan for 2–3 minutes to bring out
the flavour.
3 Grind the roasted seeds using a pestle
and mortar, then mix them into the
cheese dip.
4 Season to taste and serve with chicory
and satsuma segments.

■ CHICK PEA DIP ■

INGREDIENTS

■ 15oz (430g) can of
chick peas, drained
■ ¼ tsp cumin seeds
■ 3–4 tbsp (45–60ml)
tahini
■ 3–4 tbsp (45–60ml)
lemon juice
■ 2–3 tsp (10–15ml)
soya sauce
■ 2 cloves garlic,
crushed
■ salt and pepper

Illustrated above

The delicious nutty taste of chick peas
blends well with the accompanying
flavours. For an alternative version of this
dip, try adding herbs such as dill or chives
and reducing the soya sauce.

PREPARATION TIME: 15 mins

SERVES 4

METHOD

1 Rinse the chick peas and grind them
thoroughly in a blender or food processor.
2 Roast the cumin seeds in a dry frying
pan. Add the seeds and the remaining
ingredients to the chick peas and grind
again until fairly smooth. Season to taste.
3 Serve with cucumber, peppers and
tomatoes.

Crunchy orange dip

MUSHROOM
■ AND WALNUT DIP ■

INGREDIENTS

■ 4oz (125g) mushrooms, wiped and chopped
■ 2oz (50g) walnuts
■ 3 spring onions, trimmed and chopped
■ 1 tbsp (15ml) sunflower oil
■ 1 clove garlic, crushed
■ 1 tsp (5ml) paprika
■ 4 tsp (20ml) soya sauce
■ 1 tsp (5ml) dried marjoram
■ 4 tsp (20ml) red wine vinegar
■ 2 tbsp (30ml) tahini
■ 4–5 tbsp (60–75ml) water

Illustrated left

Mushrooms are delicious raw and add colour to dips, while walnuts contribute texture, flavour and protein. This recipe could be served with carrot and turnip crudités or be used as a savoury spread.

PREPARATION TIME: 20 mins
SERVES 4

METHOD

1 Grind the mushrooms and walnuts together in a blender or food processor.
2 Add the spring onions, oil, garlic, paprika, soya sauce, marjoram and vinegar and blend.
3 In a bowl, mix the tahini and water together until smooth.
4 Blend the diluted tahini thoroughly with the rest of the dip. Serve with crudités.

COTTAGE CHEESE
■ AND PINEAPPLE DIP ■

INGREDIENTS

■ 3oz (75g) cottage cheese
■ 2 tbsp (30ml) natural yogurt
■ 1 tbsp (15ml) mayonnaise
■ 2 tsp (10ml) sunflower oil
■ 2 tbsp (30ml) pineapple juice

Illustrated left

It is a good idea to reduce the fat content of this rich, creamy dip by using low-fat cottage cheese and low-calorie mayonnaise. To ensure a smooth, grainless result, blend all the ingredients thoroughly.

PREPARATION TIME: 15 mins
SERVES 4

METHOD

1 In a blender, mix the cottage cheese with the yogurt until very smooth.
2 Add the remaining ingredients and blend until smooth.
3 Serve with chunks of pineapple, radicchio and mangetout.

FROM TOP: Mushroom and walnut dip; Cottage cheese and pineapple dip

MUSHROOM AND
▮ WATERCRESS PÂTÉ ▮

INGREDIENTS

▪ ½oz (15g) butter or
margarine
▪ ½ onion, peeled
and finely chopped
▪ 8oz (250g) dark
mushrooms, wiped
▪ 10 juniper berries,
crushed
▪ pinch salt
▪ 4oz (125g)
watercress, chopped
▪ 2 tbsp (30ml) water
▪ 2oz (50g) shelled
pecan nuts, ground
(or 1½oz/40g
ground walnuts)
▪ salt and pepper

Illustrated below

This smooth, light pâté makes a good
low-calorie starter on toast. The slightly
resinous-tasting juniper berries
complement the pervading flavours of
mushroom and watercress.

PREPARATION TIME: 15 mins
COOKING TIME: 25 mins
SERVES 4

METHOD

1 Melt the butter in a covered saucepan
and gently fry the onion until soft. Add the
mushrooms, juniper berries and salt and
cook for a further 5 minutes.
2 Stir in the watercress and cook for a
further 2–3 minutes. Then add the water
and cook for 10 minutes. Cool, then chop
the mixture very finely. Add the pecan
nuts and seasoning. Mix well and put in a
serving dish. Allow to cool completely.
3 Serve on individual plates on a bed of
lettuce or watercress with wholemeal or
melba toast.

Mushroom and watercress pâté

Marinated aubergine

▮ MARINATED AUBERGINE ▮

INGREDIENTS

▪ 1lb (500g)
aubergine
▪ ¼ pint (150ml)
water
▪ ½ pint (300ml)
white wine vinegar

MARINADE
▪ 2 tbsp (30ml) lemon
juice
▪ 2 tbsp (30ml) extra
virgin olive oil
▪ 2 cloves garlic,
crushed
▪ 2 tsp (10ml)
chopped fresh
oregano
▪ 1 tsp (5ml) chopped
green chilli
▪ 1 tbsp (15ml)
capers
▪ salt and pepper

Illustrated above

This is a healthy adaptation of a rich
traditional Italian recipe. It makes a
strongly flavoured starter with a
surprisingly smooth texture.

PREPARATION TIME: 20 mins (plus 24 hours
marinating)
COOKING TIME: about 10 mins
SERVES 4

METHOD

1 Peel and thinly slice the aubergine
lengthways.
2 Mix the water and vinegar together in a
covered saucepan, and bring to the boil.
Add a few slices of aubergine at a time to
the pan and simmer until the colour and
texture begin to change. Drain well.
Repeat the process until all the slices are
cooked.
3 For the marinade, mix all the
ingredients together in a screw-top jar.
Add the warm aubergine and leave to
marinate for 24 hours.
4 Drain and serve cool with warm,
wholemeal toast.

■ SPICED CASHEW NUTS ■

INGREDIENTS

■ 1 tbsp (15ml) sunflower oil
■ 1 onion, peeled and finely chopped
■ 4 cloves garlic, crushed
■ 2 tsp (10ml) ground coriander
■ 1 tsp (5ml) ground cumin
■ ½ tsp turmeric
■ ½ inch (1cm) fresh root ginger, grated
■ 7oz (200g) can tomatoes
■ 4oz (125g) cashew nuts
■ 1 tsp (5ml) cumin seeds
■ 1 tsp (5ml) paprika
■ juice and rind of ½ lemon
■ pinch chilli powder
■ 2 tbsp (30ml) chopped fresh coriander
■ salt and pepper

GARNISH
■ coriander

Illustrated right

The cashew nut is delicious in savoury and sweet dishes with its creamy flavour and crunchy texture. The Indonesians, Indians and Chinese use cashew nuts to provide a contrast to rice or vegetables.
PREPARATION TIME: 25 mins
COOKING TIME: 15–20 mins
SERVES 4

METHOD

1 Heat the oil in a pan and gently fry the onion and garlic until soft.
2 Mix the coriander, cumin, turmeric and ginger into a paste using a little water. Add to the onion and garlic and cook for 2 minutes.
3 Stir in the remaining ingredients except the fresh coriander.
4 Bring to the boil and cook gently for 15–20 minutes until thoroughly heated through.
5 Stir in the fresh coriander just before serving. Season to taste.

CLOCKWISE FROM TOP LEFT: *Tofu stir-fry with coconut; Mangetout with orange sauce; Spiced cashew nuts*

MANGETOUT
■ WITH ORANGE SAUCE ■

INGREDIENTS

■ juice of 2 oranges
■ 1 tsp (5ml) grated orange rind
■ ¼ tsp ground allspice
■ 2 tsp (10ml) honey
■ 2 tbsp (30ml) cider vinegar
■ 2 tsp (10ml) arrowroot or cornflour
■ 2 tbsp (30ml) water
■ salt and pepper
■ 1lb (500g) mangetout

GARNISH
■ orange peel

Illustrated above

Sweet and delicately flavoured, mangetout peas are part of the pulse family and a good source of protein and fibre. Here they are served with a simple, spiced fruity sauce, making them a good accompaniment to a rich nut roast, or a grain dish such as savoury brown rice.
PREPARATION TIME: 10 mins
COOKING TIME: 5 mins
SERVES 4

METHOD

1 For the sauce, mix together the orange juice and rind, allspice, honey and cider vinegar.
2 Dissolve the arrowroot or cornflour in the water and add to the sauce.
3 Heat gently until boiling, stirring continuously. Simmer for 2 minutes, then season to taste.
4 Lightly steam the mangetout for 3 minutes. Serve coated with the sauce.

TOFU STIR-FRY ■ WITH COCONUT ■

INGREDIENTS

- 1oz (25g) creamed coconut
- 4 tbsp (60ml) boiling water
- 2 tsp (10ml) arrowroot or cornflour
- 2 tbsp (30ml) lemon juice
- 2 tsp (10ml) sesame oil
- 2 tsp (10ml) sunflower oil
- 2 tsp (10ml) grated fresh root ginger
- 1–2 cloves garlic, crushed
- 1 tsp (5ml) mustard seeds
- 6oz (175g) firm tofu (bean curd), thinly sliced
- 8oz (250g) broccoli florets
- 8oz (250g) carrots, cut into julienne strips

Illustrated left

This colourful combination of vegetables and tofu is easy and quick to prepare. Tofu (bean curd) is high in protein and free from cholesterol. Having little taste itself, it readily absorbs other flavours and is consequently enriched by the coconut milk.

PREPARATION TIME: 15 mins
COOKING TIME: 5–6 mins
SERVES 4

METHOD

1 Grate the creamed coconut and dissolve in the boiling water to make a thin milk. Leave to cool.
2 Mix the arrowroot or cornflour, lemon juice and sesame oil with the coconut milk and set aside.
3 Heat the sunflower oil in a wok or large frying pan and quickly fry the ginger, garlic and mustard seeds.
4 Add the tofu, broccoli and carrots and fry for 3–4 minutes, stirring constantly.
5 Pour the coconut dressing over the vegetables and cook for 2 minutes to coat the vegetables lightly. Serve immediately.

PEANUT AND SPROUT ■ STIR-FRY ■

INGREDIENTS

- 1 tbsp (15ml) sesame oil
- 2 spring onions, trimmed and chopped
- 2 cloves garlic, crushed
- 8oz (250g) Chinese leaves or spinach, shredded
- 1 large green pepper, diced
- 8oz (250g) button mushrooms
- 6–8oz (175–250g) bean sprouts
- 2oz (50g) roasted unsalted peanuts
- 4 tbsp (60ml) sherry
- 2 tbsp (30ml) soya sauce
- 2 tbsp (30ml) clear honey

Illustrated below

This stir-fry recipe is like a hot green salad – very crisp and crunchy in texture. You can buy commercially grown bean sprouts, or grow your own (see page 56)

PREPARATION TIME: 15 mins
COOKING TIME: 5 mins
SERVES 4

METHOD

1 Heat the oil in a wok or large frying pan and quickly fry the spring onions and garlic.
2 Add the Chinese leaves or spinach, pepper, mushrooms, bean sprouts and peanuts. Keep the heat high and fry these vegetables for 3–4 minutes, stirring constantly.
3 Mix the sherry, soya sauce and honey together, then pour over the vegetables. Leave for 30 seconds, season and serve immediately.

Peanut and sprout stir-fry

Mixed seed rissoles

■ MIXED SEED RISSOLES ■

INGREDIENTS

- ▌ 2oz (50g) pumpkin seeds
- ▌ 2oz (50g) sunflower seeds
- ▌ 2oz (50g) sesame seeds
- ▌ 2 sticks celery, trimmed and diced
- ▌ ¼ tsp cumin seeds
- ▌ ¼ tsp turmeric
- ▌ 4 tsp (20ml) lemon juice
- ▌ 1 tsp (5ml) soya sauce
- ▌ salt and pepper
- ▌ 3–4 tbsp (45–60ml) finely chopped fresh parsley

Illustrated above

Pumpkin, sesame and sunflower seeds make an excellent nutritional mix – high in protein, vitamins and minerals. The spices add extra flavour to the crunchy consistency of the seeds and celery.

PREPARATION TIME: 20 mins
MAKES: 4 × 2oz (50g) rissoles

METHOD

1 Grind the seeds thoroughly in a food processor or nut mill.
2 Add the celery, spices, lemon juice, soya sauce and season to taste.
3 Mix in a food processor or blender until the mixture begins to bind together.
4 Shape into rissoles and coat in fresh parsley.
5 Serve with salad, dill and slices of cucumber.

STUFFED TOMATOES WITH BULGAR WHEAT, FENNEL AND ■ PINE KERNELS ■

INGREDIENTS

- ▌ 4 large tomatoes
- ▌ 2oz (50g) bulgar wheat
- ▌ 4fl oz (125ml) water
- ▌ 6oz (175g) fennel
- ▌ 2oz (50g) pine kernels
- ▌ 1oz (25g) currants
- ▌ 2 tbsp (30ml) red wine vinegar
- ▌ 1 tbsp (15ml) olive oil
- ▌ 4 tbsp (60ml) chopped fresh parsley
- ▌ 1 tsp (5ml) soya sauce
- ▌ salt and pepper

GARNISH

- ▌ few sprigs of mint

Illustrated below

The distinctive flavour and texture of bulgar wheat makes it a useful high-fibre addition to salads and vegetable stuffings.
PREPARATION TIME: 35 mins
SERVES 4

METHOD

1 Slice a lid off each tomato and scoop out the inner flesh and seeds.
2 Put the bulgar wheat in a medium-sized bowl, boil the water and pour over the wheat. Allow to stand for 15–20 minutes.
3 Meanwhile trim and dice the fennel.
4 Mix the fennel, pine kernels, currants, vinegar, oil, parsley and soya sauce into the bulgar wheat and season to taste.
5 Fill each tomato with the mixture, garnish with a sprig of mint and serve at room temperature.

Stuffed tomatoes with bulgar wheat, fennel and pine kernels

Stuffed vine leaves with olive paste

STUFFED VINE LEAVES
■ WITH OLIVE PASTE ■

INGREDIENTS

- ■ 4oz (125g) fresh black olives
- ■ 1 tbsp (15ml) lemon juice
- ■ 2 spring onions, trimmed and chopped
- ■ 2 tomatoes, skinned and chopped
- ■ 1 tsp (5ml) dried oregano
- ■ ¼ tsp celery seeds
- ■ 1 clove garlic, crushed
- ■ 1 tbsp (15ml) chopped fresh parsley)
- ■ salt and pepper
- ■ 2–3 tbsp (30–45ml) tahini
- ■ 12–14 vine leaves

Illustrated above

A variation on a classic Greek dish, these savoury mouthfuls make a good high-fibre, low-fat meal. The strong flavour of the olive paste combines well with vine leaves and the tahini helps to offset the acidity of the other ingredients.
PREPARATION TIME: 40 mins
SERVES 4

METHOD

1 Stone the olives and chop into small pieces.
2 In a blender, mix all the ingredients except the tahini and vine leaves. Season to taste.
3 Stir in the tahini. This will thicken the mixture slightly.
4 Rinse the vine leaves. Put a heaped dessertspoon of olive paste in the centre of each leaf and roll up (see right). Serve with a wedge of lemon.

STUFFING VINE
■ LEAVES ■

*S*tuffed vine leaves, known as Dolmades in Greece and Dolmas in Turkey, are a traditional Middle-Eastern dish, in which a savoury filling is wrapped in a parcel of vine leaves and served hot or cold. The leaves are available in Britain, fresh or canned and preserved in brine. You could use blanched cabbage and spinach leaves in the same way.

1 Remove the stalk and put a dessertspoon of filling into the centre of each leaf.

2 Start folding the base and left side of the leaf over the filling.

3 Fold the right side of the leaf over the filling and roll the leaf away from you to form a neat package.

∎ SOUPS ∎

CLOCKWISE FROM TOP LEFT: Raw vegetable soup (see p.36); Raw carrot and pineapple soup (see p.36); Beetroot and orange soup (see p.36)

■ RAW VEGETABLE SOUP ■

INGREDIENTS

■ ½ bunch watercress, chopped
■ 1 large avocado, peeled, stoned and chopped
■ ½ medium green pepper, deseeded and chopped
■ 1 green dessert apple, cored and chopped
■ 12fl oz (350ml) water
■ 1 vegetable stock cube
■ 2 tbsp (30ml) lemon juice
■ 2 tsp (10ml) chopped fresh parsley or coriander

GARNISH

■ few sprigs of watercress, chopped parsley or coriander

Illustrated on page 35

This fresh green potage is best eaten as soon as it is made to conserve all the vitamins. When chopping the watercress, be sure to discard the large stalks, which taste very peppery.

PREPARATION TIME: 10–15 mins
SERVES 4

METHOD

1 Put all the soup ingredients except the parsley or coriander in a blender or food processor and mix for a few seconds until just smooth; adjust consistency if necessary.
2 Pour out of the blender into a serving bowl and stir in the parsley or coriander.
3 Garnish and serve in cool soup bowls.

■ BEETROOT AND ■ ORANGE SOUP ■

INGREDIENTS

■ 6oz (175g) raw beetroot, peeled and diced
■ ½ pint (300ml) red grape juice
■ juice of 2 large oranges
■ 4oz (125g) soured cream or smetana
■ ½ tsp ground allspice
■ salt and pepper

Illustrated on page 35

Orange and beetroot make a delicious and nutritious combination in this colourful soup.

PREPARATION TIME: 20 mins (plus chilling time)
SERVES 4

METHOD

1 In a juicer, blender or food processor, mix the beetroot and red grape juice until smooth. If you are not using a juicer, sieve the mixture through a double layer of muslin or a tea towel.
2 Blend the juice with the orange juice, soured cream and allspice for a few seconds in the washed blender or food processor. Season to taste.
3 Chill for 2–3 hours before serving.

■ RAW CARROT AND ■ PINEAPPLE SOUP ■

INGREDIENTS

■ 8oz (250g) carrots, scrubbed and diced
■ 4oz (125g) fresh pineapple flesh
■ 12fl oz (350ml) water
■ 2 tbsp (30ml) lemon juice
■ 1 pear or dessert apple, peeled, cored and diced
■ 2 tsp (10ml) chopped apple mint

GARNISH

■ a few apple mint leaves
■ pear and apple slices

Illustrated on page 35

This cool, fruity soup makes a healthy start to any meal. There are many types of mint; here apple mint adds a little sharpness to the sweet fruity flavour and makes a good garnish. When blending the carrot and pineapple, you will need to process the ingredients several times to get a smooth result.

PREPARATION TIME: 25 mins (plus chilling time)
SERVES 4

METHOD

1 In a juicer, blender or food processor, mix the carrot and pineapple together until very smooth. If you are not using a juicer, sieve the mixture through a double layer of muslin or a tea towel.
2 Add the water, lemon juice and pear or apple and blend again.
3 Transfer the soup to a bowl and add the chopped apple mint. Chill for 2–3 hours.
4 Garnish with apple mint leaves and pear or apple slices. Serve cold.

Garden soup

■ GARDEN SOUP ■

INGREDIENTS

■ 4oz (125g) green beans, trimmed and diced
■ 4oz (125g) peas
■ 6 spring onions, finely chopped
■ 14fl oz (400ml) natural yogurt, or a mixture of yogurt and single cream
■ ¼ pint (150ml) vegetable stock
■ 2 tbsp (30ml) lemon juice
■ 2 tbsp (30ml) chopped fresh coriander
■ 1 tbsp (15ml) chopped fresh mint
■ salt and pepper
■ ice cubes

Illustrated above

A refreshing, chilled yogurt soup that makes a welcome starter for a summer meal. Green beans (haricots verts) and peas are both good sources of protein and fibre, and add colour and flavour to the soup.
PREPARATION TIME: 15 mins (plus 1–2 hours chilling time)
SERVES 4

METHOD

1 Lightly steam the beans and peas for 5 minutes or until just tender. Drain and cool, reserving the cooking water for stock.
2 Mix the spring onions, yogurt, stock, lemon juice and herbs together. Add the beans and peas.
3 Chill for 1–2 hours. Season to taste and serve with an ice cube in each bowl.

CHILLED WATERMELON ■ SOUP ■

INGREDIENTS

■ ½ large watermelon (about 3lb/1.5kg in weight), deseeded
■ 4 tbsp (60ml) lemon juice
■ 4–6 cloves

GARNISH
■ a few ice cubes
■ nasturtium flowers

Illustrated below

This stunning, colourful soup makes an attractive starter for a summer evening dinner party. It is light, refreshing and low in calories. It is also quick and easy to prepare. If nasturtium flowers are not available, garnish with watercress.
PREPARATION TIME: 15 mins (plus chilling time)
SERVES 4

METHOD

1 Using a small scoop or spoon, scoop out several melon balls from the watermelon and reserve for decoration. Scoop out the rest of the flesh and put on one side.
2 Scrape the inner sides of the melon until smooth.
3 In a blender or food processor, mix the melon flesh with the lemon juice until smooth.
4 Pour the mixture into the melon shell or a dish, add the cloves and the melon balls and refrigerate.
5 Add a few ice cubes and garnish with nasturtium flowers.

Chilled watermelon soup

Egg flower soup

■ EGG FLOWER SOUP ■

INGREDIENTS

■ 1½ pints (900ml) well-flavoured light stock
■ 2 tbsp (30ml) soya sauce
■ 1 tsp (5ml) lemon juice
■ 2 tsp (10ml) fresh ginger root, peeled and grated
■ 2 eggs, beaten
■ 6 spring onions, trimmed and chopped
■ 1–2 tbsp (15–30ml) chopped fresh parsley
■ 1oz (25g) cooked sweetcorn
■ salt and pepper

Illustrated above

This is a vegetarian adaptation of a Chinese soup, in which the eggs are stirred into the soup to form strands resembling a flower. The traditional meat stock is here replaced by vegetable stock and plenty of seasoning.

PREPARATION TIME: 10 mins
COOKING TIME: 5–10 mins
SERVES 4

METHOD

1 Put the stock in a large saucepan and bring to the boil. Stir in the soya sauce, lemon juice and ginger.
2 Just before serving, pour in the beaten eggs and slowly stir into the boiling soup.
3 When the eggs have set and formed strands, remove the soup from the heat. Add the spring onions, parsley and sweetcorn. Season to taste and serve immediately.

HUNGARIAN ■ CUCUMBER SOUP ■

INGREDIENTS

■ 6fl oz (175ml) buttermilk or ordinary milk
■ 6fl oz (175ml) natural yogurt
■ ½ large or ¾ small cucumber
■ ½ tsp cider vinegar
■ ½ tsp dill seeds
■ ½ tsp fresh dill weed (or chopped chives)
■ 1 tbsp (15ml) chopped fresh mint

Illustrated below

This cooling, dill-flavoured soup, ideal for hot summer days, contains the thirst-quenching combination of yogurt and cucumber. For added taste, fibre and colour, do not peel the cucumber. Chives make a good alternative to dill weed.

PREPARATION TIME: 20 mins (plus chilling time)
SERVES 4

METHOD

1 Mix the buttermilk and yogurt together.
2 Chop half the cucumber into small cubes. Grate the remainder, using the coarser side of the grater, or the grating disc of a processor. Set on one side.
3 In a blender or food processor, mix the cubed cucumber with the cider vinegar and dill seeds until smooth. Add to the buttermilk mixture.
4 Stir in the dill weed (or chives), mint and grated cucumber, mixing well. Serve chilled. Add an ice cube on very hot days.

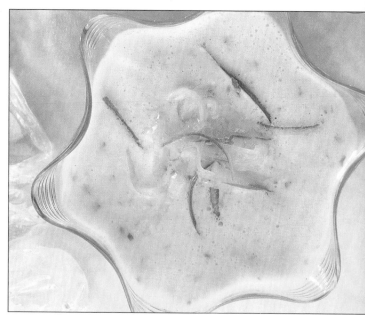

FROM LEFT: Hungarian cucumber soup; Chilled sour cherry soup

CHILLED
■ SOUR CHERRY SOUP ■

INGREDIENTS

■ 1lb (500g) Morello
cherries
■ 7fl oz (200ml) white
grape juice
■ 7fl oz (200ml)
medium-dry white
wine
■ 1 inch (2.5cm)
cinnamon stick
■ rind and juice of
½ lemon
■ 5oz (150g) carton
natural yogurt
■ 2 tbsp (30ml)
soured cream

GARNISH

■ 2 tbsp (30ml)
soured cream

Illustrated below

Dark, plump Morello cherries provide the
best colour and flavour for this soup.

PREPARATION TIME: 20 mins (plus chilling
time)

COOKING TIME: 15 mins

SERVES 4

METHOD

1 Remove the cherry stalks and put on one
side. Prepare the cherries (see right).
2 Add the grape juice, wine, cinnamon,
lemon rind and juice to the cherry stalks
and stones and cook (see right). Strain and
reserve the liquid.
3 Blend the cherries with the liquid (see
right) in a blender or food processor. Pour
in the yogurt and soured cream and
process for another few seconds. Leave to
cool, then cover and refrigerate until ready
to serve.
4 Serve chilled, garnished with some
cherries (optional) and a swirl of soured
cream.

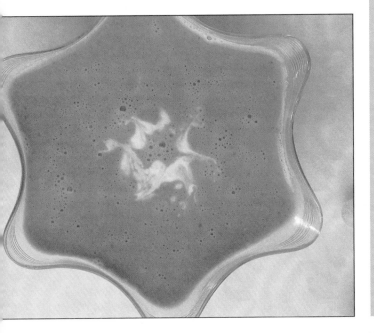

MAKING A
■ CHERRY SAUCE ■

*T*here are several hundred varieties of cherry.
The best-known sour cherries are morellos (with
dark or light skins) and amarelles (with red skins). A
basic cherry purée is extremely versatile and can be used
as the base for a soup, as here, as a topping for fruit
desserts, pancakes or healthy ice creams, or as a base for
sauces or mousses. Cherries have rather a short season,
but you can use canned or frozen ones.

*1 Stone the cherries using either
a cherry stoner or the tip of a
pointed knife, and set on one side.*

*2 Simmer the stalks and stones
with the liquids for 5 minutes.
Cool, then strain and blend until
smooth.*

*3 Combine the cherry purée with
the yogurt and soured cream
(shown left). Process for a few
more seconds.*

Celery and tomato soup

Soup Chinese style

CELERY AND
■ TOMATO SOUP ■

INGREDIENTS

■ 1 tbsp (15ml) olive oil
■ 1 onion, peeled and finely chopped
■ 6 sticks celery, trimmed and chopped
■ 1 clove garlic, crushed
■ pinch salt
■ 6 large tomatoes, skinned, deseeded and chopped
■ 1 tbsp (15ml) chopped fresh parsley
■ 1 tbsp (15ml) fresh basil
■ 1 pint (600ml) stock or water
■ salt and pepper

Illustrated above

This strongly flavoured, colourful soup makes a great summer starter and is delicious served with fresh wholemeal bread (see p. 118). The tomatoes can be deseeded, but leaving them whole increases the fibre content. A garnish of chopped fresh parsley goes well with this soup.

PREPARATION TIME: 15 mins
COOKING TIME: 25 mins
SERVES 4

METHOD

1 Heat the oil in a large saucepan and gently fry the onion.
2 Add the celery and garlic, sprinkle them with a pinch of salt to bring out the juices and cook for 10 minutes.
3 Add the tomatoes to the pan with the parsley, basil and stock. Simmer for 15 minutes.
4 Season to taste and serve.

■ SOUP CHINESE STYLE ■

INGREDIENTS

■ 2 tsp (10ml) sesame oil
■ 1 inch (2.5cm) piece of fresh root ginger, peeled and grated
■ ½ onion, peeled and sliced
■ 2oz (50g) mushrooms, wiped and sliced
■ 1¾ pints (1 litre) stock
■ 2 leaves Chinese leaf, shredded
■ 2 inch (5cm) mooli, peeled and thinly sliced
■ 1oz (25g) Chinese noodles
■ 4oz (125g) tofu (bean curd), cut into strips
■ 2oz (50g) bean sprouts
■ 2 tsp–1 tbsp (10–15ml) soya sauce

Illustrated above

The rich variety of oriental vegetables gives this soup an exotic appeal and a good balance of essential nutrients. The tofu (bean curd) adds protein and a smooth texture, while the ginger and soya sauce contribute to the subtle flavours. Mooli, a large white radish, is also known as daikon or Japanese white radish.

PREPARATION TIME: 15 mins
COOKING TIME: 10 mins
SERVES 4

METHOD

1 Heat the oil in a heavy-based saucepan and fry the ginger and onion for 1–2 minutes.
2 Add the mushrooms and cook for a further 2 minutes. Add the stock and bring to the boil. Stir in the Chinese leaves and the mooli and cook for 3–4 minutes.
3 Add the noodles, tofu and bean sprouts, bring back to the boil and remove from the heat. Stir in the soya sauce, cover and leave to stand for 6 minutes before serving.

CELERIAC SOUP
▌ WITH LEMON ▐

INGREDIENTS

- ¼ onion, peeled and chopped
- 1lb (500g) celeriac, peeled and chopped
- rind of ½ lemon
- ½ tsp ground white mustard seeds
- 2fl oz (50ml) dry white wine
- 1¼ pints (750ml) light stock or water
- 2 tbsp (30ml) lemon juice
- 1 tsp (5ml) finely chopped fresh parsley or coriander
- salt and pepper

GARNISH
- Sprigs of fresh parsley or coriander
- 1 tsp (5ml) lemon rind

Illustrated below

Add the parsley or coriander just before serving, or the flavour may be too strong.

PREPARATION TIME: 15 mins

COOKING TIME: 35 mins

SERVES 4

METHOD

1 Put the onion, celeriac, lemon rind, mustard seed, white wine and stock in a medium saucepan.
2 Bring to the boil and simmer for about 30 minutes. Purée in a blender or food processor until just smooth.
3 Pour the soup into a clean saucepan and add the lemon juice, chopped parsley or coriander and seasoning. Simmer for 2 minutes. Serve hot, garnished with sprigs of parsley or coriander and a sprinkling of lemon rind.

Spinach and broccoli soup with tarragon

SPINACH AND BROCCOLI
▌ SOUP WITH TARRAGON ▐

INGREDIENTS

- 1lb (500g) broccoli, roughly chopped
- 8oz (250g) spinach, roughly chopped
- 1 pint (600ml) light stock or water
- 1tsp (5ml) green peppercorns, crushed
- 2 tsp (10ml) yeast extract
- 2 tsp (10ml) chopped fresh tarragon
- 2 tbsp (30ml) chopped chives
- salt and pepper

GARNISH
- 2 tbsp (30ml) chopped chives or a few steamed broccoli florets

Illustrated above

Packed with vitamins and minerals, this soup makes a healthy start to a meal at any time of year. When fresh spinach is not available, use frozen and, if necessary, substitute calabrese for broccoli. For a splash of contrasting colour, serve with a swirl of single cream or natural yogurt.

PREPARATION TIME: 20 mins

COOKING TIME: 15 mins

SERVES 4

METHOD

1 Put the broccoli, spinach and stock in a large saucepan. Bring to the boil and simmer for 10 minutes or until the vegetables are tender. Leave to cool.
2 Purée in a blender or food processor for a few seconds and reheat gently.
3 Add the peppercorns to the soup with the yeast extract, tarragon and chives. Season to taste.
4 Simmer for a further 2–3 minutes. Garnish with chives or lightly steamed broccoli florets.

Celeriac soup with lemon

▮ TOFU AND TOMATO SOUP ▮

INGREDIENTS

- 1 large red pepper
- 1lb (500g) tomatoes
- 5oz (150g) silken tofu (bean curd)
- ¼ tsp Tabasco sauce
- pinch salt

GARNISH
- chopped fresh parsley

Illustrated right

Silken tofu (bean curd) is an ideal low-fat base for a smooth soup.

PREPARATION TIME: 20 mins (plus chilling time)

SERVES 4

METHOD

1 Blanch the pepper in boiling water for 10–15 minutes or until the skin comes off easily. Deseed and chop. Blanch the tomatoes in boiling water. Skin and chop.

2 Purée the pepper and tomatoes with all the other ingredients in a blender or food processor until smooth; adjust consistency if necessary. Chill.

3 If the soup begins to "set", process for a few seconds just before serving.

▮ CAULIFLOWER AND ▮ ▮ CORIANDER SOUP ▮

INGREDIENTS

- 1 cauliflower
- 1oz (25g) butter or margarine
- 1 onion, peeled and finely chopped
- 1 tsp (5ml) celery seeds
- 1 tsp (5ml) ground coriander
- 2 bay leaves
- 1 bouquet garni
- pinch salt
- 1½ pints (900ml) semi-skimmed milk
- ½ tsp Dijon mustard
- salt and pepper

Illustrated on page 43

This creamy soup tastes best if you use a fresh and tender cauliflower and serve it as soon as it is ready.

PREPARATION TIME: 15 mins

COOKING TIME: 35 mins

SERVES 4

METHOD

1 Chop some of the cauliflower stalk and all the florets into small pieces.

2 Melt the butter in a large saucepan and gently fry the onion and cubed cauliflower stalk, covered, for 5 minutes, without letting them brown.

3 Add the celery seeds, coriander, bay leaves, bouquet garni and a pinch of salt. Cook for 5 minutes, stirring occasionally.

4 Add the chopped florets and milk, bring to the boil and simmer for 20 minutes. Remove the bay leaves and bouquet garni. Cool slightly.

5 Purée in a blender or food processor for a few seconds until creamy. Reheat in a clean saucepan. Stir in the mustard and seasoning and simmer for 2–3 minutes. Serve as soon as possible.

FROM LEFT: Leek and potato soup; Tofu and tomato soup

▮ LEEK AND POTATO SOUP ▮

INGREDIENTS

- 1oz (25g) butter or margarine
- 4oz (125g) shallots or a small onion, peeled and chopped
- 1lb (500g) leeks, chopped
- 8oz (250g) potatoes, scrubbed and diced
- 1 bouquet garni
- 1 pint (600ml) stock or water
- ¼ pint (150ml) dry white wine
- 1 vegetable stock cube
- 2 tsp (10ml) lemon juice
- ½ tsp grated nutmeg
- 4 tbsp (60ml) chopped fresh parsley

GARNISH
- 1 tbsp (15ml) chopped fresh chives

Illustrated above

This dry, white, warming soup is good on cold autumn evenings. The wine helps to lighten the flavour of the sweet vegetables. Clean the leeks carefully before use to remove any grit.

PREPARATION TIME: 20 mins

COOKING TIME: 35 mins

SERVES 4

METHOD

1 Melt the butter in a saucepan and gently fry the shallots for 1–2 minutes. Add the leeks and potatoes and fry for another 2–3 minutes.

2 Add the bouquet garni, stock, white wine and stock cube. Bring to the boil and simmer for 25 minutes or until the potatoes are cooked. Cool slightly and remove the bouquet garni.

3 Purée in a blender or food processor until smooth.

4 Reheat gently in a clean saucepan with the lemon juice, nutmeg and chopped parsley. Bring to the boil and simmer for 1–2 minutes. Garnish with chives and serve with grated cheese.

CURRIED BEAN AND
■ MARROW SOUP ■

FROM LEFT: *Fennel soup with aniseed; Cauliflower and coriander soup*

FENNEL SOUP
■ WITH ANISEED ■

INGREDIENTS

■ 10–12oz (300–375g) fennel bulb
■ ½oz (15g) butter or margarine
■ 1 medium onion, peeled and chopped
■ 1 tsp (5ml) aniseeds
■ 1 bay leaf
■ 2 sticks celery, trimmed and chopped
■ 1¼ pints (750ml) light stock or water
■ salt and white pepper

GARNISH
■ chopped fennel leaves

Illustrated above

Aniseed, fennel and celery have complementary flavours and textures and in this recipe are combined to make a light, fresh-tasting starter. Try to find a fennel bulb that still has its leaves, to use as a garnish.

PREPARATION TIME: 10 mins
COOKING TIME: 35 mins
SERVES 4

METHOD

1 Cut off the feathery tops from the fennel and remove any damaged outside stalks. Wash the bulb and drain. Cut off the hard base, cut into quarters lengthwise and then chop across.
2 Melt the butter or margarine in a saucepan and gently fry the onion. Add the aniseeds and bay leaf and cook for 5 minutes. Stir in the fennel and celery and cook for a further 10 minutes.
3 Pour in the stock, bring to the boil and simmer for 15 minutes in a covered pan. Remove the bay leaf. Leave to cool. In a blender or food processor, purée until smooth.
4 Reheat, season, garnish and serve hot.

INGREDIENTS

■ 2oz (50g) dried black eye beans, soaked, or 8oz (250g) canned beans, drained
■ 1¼ pints (750ml) water
■ 2 tbsp (30ml) sunflower oil
■ 1 medium onion, peeled and chopped
■ 2 tsp (10ml) garam masala
■ 6 fresh curry leaves, chopped or 2 dried curry leaves, crumbled
■ 2 bay leaves
■ 2 sticks celery, chopped
■ 1 medium carrot, scrubbed and diced
■ 1lb (500g) marrow, peeled, deseeded and cubed
■ 2 large tomatoes, skinned and diced
■ 1 vegetable stock cube
■ 2oz (50g) sultanas
■ salt and pepper

Illustrated on page 44

Beans are ideal in soups, providing substance and texture. Combine them with curry spices and fresh marrow for a heart-warming dish. You can speed up the preparation and cooking time by using canned beans, in which case omit step 1.

PREPARATION TIME: 25 mins (plus 12 hours minimum soaking)
COOKING TIME: 1 hour (plus 1-2 hours for the dried black eye beans)
SERVES 4

METHOD

1 Drain the dried, soaked beans. Place in a saucepan with 1¼ pints (750ml) fresh water and simmer for 1–2 hours until soft. Drain but reserve the cooking water.
2 Heat 1 tbsp (15ml) of the oil in a saucepan and fry the onion. Add half the garam masala, curry leaves, bay leaves, celery and carrot. Cook for 5–10 minutes. Stir in the marrow, drained beans and the tomatoes and cook for a further 2–3 minutes.
3 Make up the reserved cooking water to 1¼ pints (750ml) (or use all plain water if using canned beans) and add it to the saucepan. Crumble the vegetable stock cube into the saucepan and add the sultanas. Cook for 45 minutes.
4 Gently heat the remaining oil in a small pan and fry the rest of the garam masala for 1–2 minutes, until a spicy aroma rises. Add to the soup and cook for another 5 minutes. Season and serve hot.

■ MANY BEAN SOUP ■

INGREDIENTS

- 1oz (25g) red kidney beans, soaked
- 1oz (25g) aduki beans, soaked
- 1oz (25g) mung beans, soaked
- 1oz (25g) pinto beans, soaked
- 1oz (25g) blackeye beans, soaked
- 1oz (25g) flageolet beans, soaked
- 1 tbsp (15ml) sunflower oil
- 1 onion, peeled and chopped
- ½ tsp caraway seeds
- ¼ tsp cardamom seeds, lightly crushed
- ¼ tsp aniseeds, lightly crushed
- 1 carrot, scrubbed and sliced
- 6oz (175g) leeks, chopped
- 2 tsp (10ml) chopped fresh mint
- 1 tsp (5ml) lemon juice
- salt and pepper

Illustrated right

Made with six different pulses, this soup has an instant appeal. To save weighing out small quantities of beans buy a bag of ready mixed dried beans. Caraway and aniseeds bring a nice, sharp flavour to the dish.

PREPARATION TIME: 20 mins (plus 12 hours minimum soaking)

COOKING TIME: 1½ hours

SERVES 4

METHOD

1 Drain the beans and place in a saucepan with plenty of fresh water. Boil fast for 10 minutes, then simmer for about 50 minutes.

2 Heat the oil in a medium saucepan and fry the onion until soft. Add all the seeds and cook for 1–2 minutes. Stir in the carrot and leeks and fry until both have softened.

3 Drain the cooked beans, reserving 2 pints (1.2 litres) of the stock. Add the beans and stock to the saucepan and cook for 25 minutes or until the stock has thickened.

4 Stir in the mint and the lemon juice and cook for another 2–3 minutes. Season and serve hot.

CLOCKWISE FROM TOP LEFT: Curried bean and marrow soup (see p.43); Spiced lentil soup with coconut; Brown lentil and mushroom soup; Many bean soup; Sweet potato and avocado soup

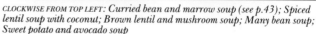

SPICED LENTIL SOUP
■ WITH COCONUT ■

INGREDIENTS

- 1 tbsp (15ml) sunflower oil
- 2 medium onions, peeled and chopped
- 1 clove garlic, crushed
- 1 bay leaf
- 1 tsp (5ml) grated fresh root ginger
- 2 tsp (10ml) turmeric
- ½ tsp cumin seeds, crushed
- ½ tsp coriander seeds, crushed
- 1 tsp (5ml) white mustard seeds, crushed
- 8oz (250g) red split lentils
- 1½ pints (900ml) water
- 1oz (25g) creamed coconut, grated
- 1 tsp (5ml) lemon juice
- salt and pepper

GARNISH
- 4 slices of lemon, cut into twists

Illustrated left

A variation on a Middle Eastern recipe, this soup derives nutritional value from the lentils, which are a good, cheap source of protein and fibre and do not need soaking before cooking. The spices give the dish an attractive appearance and a slightly hot taste. For the best flavour, grind your own spices in a good processor or a small electric grinder.

PREPARATION TIME: 20 mins
COOKING TIME: 20 mins
SERVES 4

METHOD

1 Heat the oil in a large saucepan and gently fry the onion, covered, until soft. Add the garlic, bay leaf, half the grated ginger, the turmeric, cumin, coriander and mustard seeds. Fry for a further 1–2 minutes.
2 Add the red split lentils and cook for 1 minute, stirring. Pour in the water, bring to the boil and simmer for 15 minutes.
3 Give the soup a good stir, add the rest of the grated ginger and cook for another 5 minutes.
4 Stir in the coconut, lemon juice and seasoning.
5 When the coconut is dissolved, bring up to boiling point, then remove the bay leaf. Serve hot, garnish with twists of lemon.

BROWN LENTIL AND
■ MUSHROOM SOUP ■

INGREDIENTS

- 1 tbsp (15ml) sunflower or olive oil
- 1 onion, peeled and finely chopped
- 2 cloves garlic, crushed
- 8oz (250g) mushrooms, chopped
- 8oz (250g) brown lentils
- 1–2 tbsp (30ml) fresh mixed herbs, chopped
- 1¾ pints (1 litre) dark stock or water
- 1 tsp (5ml) yeast extract
- 1 tbsp (15ml) chopped fresh parsley
- salt and pepper

Illustrated left

This is a warming, filling soup on a cold evening, and when served with garlic bread can make a complete meal. Lentils are an excellent source of protein and give the soup substance.

PREPARATION TIME: 20 mins
COOKING TIME: 1 hour
SERVES 4

METHOD

1 Heat the oil in a heavy-based saucepan and fry the onion and garlic until tender. Add the mushrooms and fry for a further 5 minutes. Add the lentils and herbs. Stir the ingredients for another 2–3 minutes.
2 Mix in the stock and yeast extract, bring to the boil and simmer for 50 minutes.
3 Season to taste and sprinkle on the chopped parsley. Simmer for another 2–3 minutes and serve.

SWEET POTATO AND
■ AVOCADO SOUP ■

INGREDIENTS

- 1lb (500g) sweet potatoes, scrubbed
- 1½ pints (900ml) water
- 1 small onion, peeled and finely chopped
- 1 ripe avocado, peeled and stoned
- grated rind and juice of ½ lemon
- grated rind and juice of 1 large orange
- ½ tsp ground mace
- pinch salt

GARNISH
- few avocado slices

Illustrated left

The colour of the soup will be determined by the type of sweet potato used.

PREPARATION TIME: 15 mins
COOKING TIME: 20 mins
SERVES 4

METHOD

1 Cut any woody parts off the sweet potatoes. Peel and dice.
2 Bring the water to the boil in a saucepan, add the potatoes and onion and simmer for about 15 minutes. Cool slightly.
3 Mix the avocado flesh and the potato and stock mixture in a blender or food processor until smooth. Reheat the soup in a clean saucepan, adding the rind and juice of the lemon and orange, the mace and a pinch of salt. Simmer for 1–2 minutes.
4 Garnish with avocado slices and serve.

Mushroom soup with a pastry lid

MUSHROOM SOUP
■ WITH A PASTRY LID ■

INGREDIENTS

■ 1oz (25g) butter or margarine
■ 1 onion, peeled and chopped
■ 12oz (375g) oyster mushrooms, chopped
■ 1 tbsp (15ml) fresh dill, chopped
■ 1 pint (600ml) dark stock(see p.49)
■ 1 tsp (5ml) yeast extract
■ 2 tsp (10ml) medium-dry sherry
■ salt and pepper

PASTRY

■ 6oz (175g) wholemeal plain flour
■ pinch salt
■ 1 tsp (5ml) dill seeds
■ 3oz (75g) butter
■ 2 tsp (10ml) sunflower oil
■ 2–3 tbsp (30–45ml) water

GLAZE

■ beaten egg

Illustrated above

The "pastry lid" on each individual bowl makes a delicious and substantial garnish.

PREPARATION TIME: 50 mins
COOKING TIME: 20–25 mins
SERVES 4

METHOD

1 Melt the butter in a saucepan and fry the onion for 2–3 minutes. Add the mushrooms and dill and fry for a further 5 minutes. Stir in the stock, yeast extract and sherry. Cook for a further 10 minutes or until the mushrooms are tender. Season and leave to cool. Purée in a blender or food processor for a few seconds. Pour into 4 ovenproof soup bowls.
2 For the pastry, mix the flour with the salt and dill. Rub in the butter until the mixture resembles breadcrumbs. Mix oil and water and add two-thirds to the flour mixture. Form into a medium-soft dough, adding the remaining oil and water if necessary. Leave the dough for 10 minutes.
3 Prepare the pastry lids (see right). Glaze with beaten egg. Bake in a preheated oven at Gas Mark 6, 400°F, 200°C for 20–25 minutes.

MAKING A
■ PASTRY LID ■

*P*astry, not known for its nutritional qualities, can nevertheless be made healthier by using less fat, switching from refined flour to wholemeal flour, or by making an egg-free variety. A pastry lid on a warming soup can provide the carbohydrate and protein necessary for a well-balanced meal.

1 Take a quarter of the pastry and roll into 4 thin strips. Dampen the rims of the serving bowls and press a strip onto each.

2 Divide the rest of the pastry into four pieces, and roll out each quarter fairly thickly to form a lid.

3 Dampen the pastry rims and place the lids on top of the serving bowls. Press down the sides to seal.

VEGETABLE SOUP
■ WITH PESTO ■

FROM LEFT: Mexican gumbo; Vegetable soup with pesto

■ MEXICAN GUMBO ■

INGREDIENTS

■ 4–6 oz (125–175g) red kidney beans, soaked, or a 15oz (430g) can
■ 1 tbsp (15ml) olive oil
■ 1 onion, peeled and finely chopped
■ 2 tsp (10ml) paprika
■ pinch chilli powder
■ pinch ground allspice
■ 1 red pepper, deseeded and diced
■ 1 green pepper, deseeded and diced
■ 10oz (300g) sweet potatoes, scrubbed and cubed
■ 4oz (125g) okra, chopped
■ 1½ pints (900ml) stock or water
■ 1 tbsp (15ml) tomato purée
■ salt and pepper

Illustrated above

This spicy, high-fibre soup derives its name from okra, also known as gumbo. If using dried beans use the cooking water as stock, it will add flavour and minerals. If using canned beans, omit step 1 and make stock from water and a stock cube.
PREPARATION TIME: 25 mins (plus 12 hours minimum soaking)
COOKING TIME: 1 hour 40 mins
SERVES 4

METHOD

1 Drain the beans. Place in a saucepan with plenty of fresh water and boil fast for 10 minutes, then simmer for about 50 minutes until tender. Drain and reserve the stock.
2 Heat the oil in a saucepan and gently fry the onion. Add the spices and fry for 1–2 minutes, until a roasted aroma rises.
3 Stir in the peppers, cubed sweet potatoes and drained beans and cook over a medium heat for 3–5 minutes. Add the okra and the reserved stock. Bring to the boil and simmer for 30 minutes.
4 Stir in the tomato purée and seasoning and cook for a further 5 minutes. Serve hot.

INGREDIENTS

■ 1½ tsp (7.5ml) olive oil
■ ½ large onion, peeled and chopped
■ 1–2 cloves garlic, crushed
■ 1 tsp (5ml) fresh basil
■ ½ red pepper, deseeded and chopped
■ 4oz (125g) green beans, chopped
■ 2oz (50g) wholemeal macaroni
■ 1¼ pints (750ml) tomato
■ a quantity of stock (see p.49)
■ 1 vegetable stock cube
■ 6–8oz (175–250g) cherry tomatoes
■ salt and pepper

PESTO

■ 1–2 cloves garlic, crushed
■ 1½oz (40g) fresh basil
■ 2oz (50g) skimmed milk soft cheese
■ 1oz (25g) toasted pine nuts, ground
■ 1oz (25g) grated Parmesan cheese or Pecorino

Illustrated left

This low-fat version of pesto, a traditional Italian sauce, uses skimmed milk soft cheese instead of olive oil. The result is a delicious soup with a strong basil flavour. Use half the quantity of dried basil if you cannot get fresh. If cherry tomatoes are not available, use quartered tomatoes.
PREPARATION TIME: 30 mins
COOKING TIME: 35 mins
SERVES 4

METHOD

1 Heat the oil in a large saucepan and fry the onion until transparent. Add the garlic and basil, cover and cook for a further 1–2 minutes.
2 Stir in the pepper, green beans and macaroni, coating them in the oil.
3 Add the stock and crumbled stock cube, bring to the boil and simmer for 15–20 minutes or until the macaroni and beans are cooked. Add the tomatoes and simmer for a further 5 minutes. Season to taste.
4 Prepare the pesto (see p.48). Pour the hot soup over the pesto, stir to melt the cheese and serve immediately.

■ MAKING PESTO ■

*P*esto is a traditional Italian sauce made from basil and garlic, originally from Genoa. It can be used as a sauce to accompany pasta or jacket potatoes or rice, and also works well as a base for soup. Garlic, a member of the onion family, is renowned for its benefits to the digestive system.

1 Crush 1–2 garlic cloves into a mixing bowl.

2 Mix with fresh basil, skimmed milk soft cheese, ground toasted pine nuts and Parmesan cheese to form a paste.

3 Place in a dish and pour hot soup over it. If using as a sauce, heat in a pan until the cheese melts, then serve.

FARM SOUP WITH ■ SUNFLOWER SEEDS ■

INGREDIENTS

■ 1 tbsp (15ml) sunflower oil
■ 1 onion, peeled and finely chopped
■ 2oz (50g) parsnips, peeled and diced
■ 1 bay leaf
■ 6oz (175g) small cauliflower florets
■ 5oz (150g) runner beans, chopped
■ 8oz (250g) red split lentils
■ 1¾ pints (1 litre) light stock
■ 1 tsp (5ml) fresh rosemary
■ 1 tbsp (15ml) chopped fresh parsley
■ 2oz (50g) sunflower seeds
■ salt and pepper

Illustrated below

Lentils always make for a good, hearty soup. This one is no exception. It contains a mixture of seeds, vegetables and pulses, and produces a very filling soup.

PREPARATION TIME: 45 mins
COOKING TIME: 50–60 mins
SERVES 4

METHOD

1 Heat the oil in a large saucepan and fry the onion, parsnips and bay leaf until the onion is soft.
2 Mix in the cauliflower florets and runner beans and cook for 5 minutes. Mix in the red split lentils, stock, rosemary and parsley and cook for 15 minutes.
3 Stir the soup thoroughly and cook for 20 minutes. Add the sunflower seeds and cook for a further 10 minutes. Remove the bay leaf. Season to taste and serve.

Farm soup with sunflower seeds

■ BASIC LIGHT STOCK ■

INGREDIENTS

■ 2 pints (1.2 litres) water
■ ½ onion, peeled and chopped
■ 1 medium carrot, scrubbed and chopped
■ handful celery leaves
■ few black peppercorns

Illustrated right

Stocks form a useful starch-free base for soups, adding flavour and colour as well as body. This recipe makes a simple, clear stock. Any vegetable scraps or peelings can be added, such as leeks, green beans, celeriac, mooli, etc. – but don't use any brassicas, e.g. cabbage, broccoli, cauliflower, as their strong flavour may taint the stock and they can affect its keeping qualities. To make a tomato-flavoured stock, add 2 tsp (10ml) tomato purée.

PREPARATION TIME: 5 mins
COOKING TIME: 1 hour 30 mins
MAKES: 1½ pints (900ml)

METHOD

1 Place all the ingredients in a medium saucepan.
2 Bring to the boil and simmer uncovered for 1½ hours. Strain and use.

■ DARK STOCK ■

INGREDIENTS

■ ¼oz (7g) dried mushrooms
■ 2 pints (1.2 litres) cold water
■ 2 tsp (10ml) sunflower oil
■ skins of 3–4 onions
■ 1 medium carrot, peeled and diced
■ few black peppercorns

Illustrated right

A combination of dried mushrooms and onion skins makes an excellent dark stock that is useful for giving savoury dishes extra flavour and depth of colour.

PREPARATION TIME: 10 mins
COOKING TIME: 1 hour 25 mins
MAKES: 1½ pints (900ml)

METHOD

1 Soak the mushrooms in the cold water for a few minutes.
2 Meanwhile fry the onion skins in the oil in a heavy-based saucepan.
3 After 2–3 minutes, add the mushrooms together with the soaking water.
4 Add the carrot and peppercorns, bring to the boil and simmer for 1¼ hours.
5 Strain and use within two days.

FROM TOP: Dark stock; Basic light stock

■ QUICK STOCKS ■

The following are quick and easy methods of making stock. Some may change the colour of the soup, so choose your method carefully.

■ **1** Dissolve 1 tsp (5ml) vegetable concentrate in 1 pint (600ml) hot water.

■ **2** Dissolve 1 tsp (5ml) yeast extract in 1 pint (600ml) hot water.

■ **3** Dissolve 1 vegetable stock cube in 1 pint (600ml) hot water.

■ **4** Add 2 tsp (10ml) soya sauce to 1 pint (600ml) water.

▪ SALADS ▪

CLOCKWISE FROM TOP LEFT: Flageolet and orange salad with fresh herbs (see p.52); Lentil and orange salad (see p.52); Bean sprout salad (see p.52)

■ BEAN SPROUT SALAD ■

INGREDIENTS

■ 8oz (250g) bean
sprouts, preferably a
mixture of mung
bean sprouts and
aduki bean sprouts.
■ 4 sticks celery,
trimmed and diced
■ 6oz (175g) Chinese
leaves, shredded
■ 8oz (250g) carrots,
scrubbed and grated
■ 2oz (50g) raisins

DRESSING

■ 2 tbsp (30ml) soya
sauce
■ 2 tbsp (30ml) lemon
juice
■ 2 tsp (10ml) honey
■ 1 tsp (5ml) grated
fresh root ginger
■ 2 tbsp (30ml)
sesame oil
■ salt and pepper

Illustrated on page 51

You can buy commercially grown bean
sprouts, but growing your own (see p.56) is
very easy and allows you to combine
different varieties in interesting and
colourful salads. The complementary
flavours of soya sauce, ginger and lemon
make an excellent dressing.

PREPARATION TIME: 20 mins

SERVES 4

METHOD

1 Rinse the bean sprouts and mix together
in a bowl.
2 Add the celery, Chinese leaves, carrots
and raisins and mix well.
3 For the dressing, mix all the ingredients
together and season to taste.
4 Pour the dressing over the salad, toss,
and serve.

■ LENTIL AND
ORANGE SALAD ■

INGREDIENTS

■ 3oz (75g) brown
lentils
■ ¼ pint (150ml)
natural yogurt
■ juice of 1 orange
■ 1 tbsp (15ml)
sesame seeds
■ 1 tsp (5ml) cumin
seeds
■ salt and pepper
■ 6oz (175g) fresh
spinach, washed and
chopped
■ 2 satsumas, peeled
and segmented

Illustrated on page 51

Lentils contain lots of protein and fibre.
They are also easy to digest and make a
tasty salad ingredient.

PREPARATION TIME: 10 mins

COOKING TIME: 30–40 mins for the lentils

SERVES 4

METHOD

1 Bring the lentils to the boil in plenty of
fresh water and cook for 30–40 minutes or
until soft. Drain well and cool.
2 Mix the yogurt and orange juice
together.
3 Lightly toast the sesame and cumin
seeds in a dry frying pan for 3–4 minutes.
Add to the yogurt. Mix in the lentils.
Season.
4 Arrange the chopped spinach and
satsuma segments on a large plate and pile
the lentil mixture in the centre.

FLAGEOLET AND
ORANGE SALAD WITH
■ FRESH HERBS ■

INGREDIENTS

SALAD

■ 6oz (175g) dried
flageolet beans,
soaked, or 15oz
(430g) can
■ 1 bunch spring
onions, sliced
■ 2 oranges, peeled
and segmented
■ 2 tbsp (30ml)
chopped fresh
coriander
■ 2 tbsp (30ml)
chopped fresh parsley
■ 12 stuffed green
olives, sliced

DRESSING

■ juice of ½ orange
■ 2 tbsp (30ml) lemon
juice
■ 1 tsp (5ml) extra
virgin olive oil
■ 1 tsp (5ml) cider
vinegar
■ salt and pepper

Illustrated on page 51

Flageolet beans have a sweet, delicate
flavour that blends perfectly with citrus
fruits, herbs and onions. The beans
provide substance, while the other
ingredients add moisture and flavour.
If using canned beans, omit step 1 of the
method.

PREPARATION TIME: 10 mins (plus 10–12
hours soaking time)

COOKING TIME: 40–50 mins for the beans

SERVES 4

METHOD

1 Drain the beans. Bring to the boil in
plenty of fresh water. Boil fast for 10
minutes, reduce the heat and simmer for
30–40 minutes or until the beans are soft.
2 Mix the dressing ingredients together
and season well.
3 Drain the beans well and mix into the
dressing. Leave to cool.
4 Prepare the spring onions and oranges.
Mix them with the cooled beans, herbs and
olives. Serve chilled.

Barbecued bean salad

FROM LEFT: Cucumber stuffed with cottage cheese; Stuffed iceberg lettuce with pecans and cheese (see p.54)

■ BARBECUED BEAN SALAD ■

INGREDIENTS

- 6oz (175g) black or red kidney beans, soaked or a 15oz (430g) can red kidney beans, drained
- 1 tbsp (15ml) olive oil
- 1 red onion, peeled and finely chopped
- 1 clove garlic, crushed
- 1 tbsp (15ml) red wine vinegar
- 7oz (200g) can tomatoes, chopped
- 2fl oz (50ml) apple juice
- 2 slices lemon
- sprig thyme and 1 bay leaf
- 4oz (125g) button mushrooms, halved
- 1 green pepper, deseeded and diced
- salt and pepper

Illustrated left

There are two well-known types of kidney bean; the black is the sweeter of the two, but the red canned variety can also be used, in which case omit step 1 of the method.

PREPARATION TIME: 10 mins (plus 10–12 hours soaking time)

COOKING TIME: 25 mins (plus 40–50 mins for the beans)

SERVES 4

METHOD

1 Drain the beans. Bring to the boil in plenty of fresh water. Boil fast for 10 minutes, then cover and simmer for 30–40 minutes.

2 Heat the oil in a pan and gently fry the onion and garlic until soft. Add the vinegar, tomatoes, apple juice, lemon, thyme and bay leaf. Bring to the boil and simmer for 20 minutes.

3 Stir in the drained beans and the mushrooms and cook for 5 minutes. Remove the lemon, thyme and bay leaf. Leave to cool. Add the green pepper. Season to taste.

CUCUMBER STUFFED WITH ■ COTTAGE CHEESE ■

INGREDIENTS

- 4oz (125g) cottage cheese
- 1 tbsp (15ml) lemon juice
- 1 tsp (5ml) fresh basil
- ¼ tsp fennel seeds
- ½ tsp fresh rosemary
- ¼ tsp turmeric
- salt and pepper
- 1 large cucumber

GARNISH
- watercress sprigs

Illustrated above

A combination of herbs adds an exciting flavour to cottage cheese. Put the mixture in a cucumber case to make a light salad meal.

PREPARATION TIME: 30 mins

SERVES 4

METHOD

1 In a blender or food processor, mix together the cottage cheese, lemon juice, herbs and spices. Season to taste.

2 Slice the cucumber in half along its length and scoop out the seeds from the centre.

3 Fill the hollow with the cheese mixture and slice into 2 inch (5cm) chunks.

4 Serve with a few sprigs of watercress.

STUFFED ICEBERG LETTUCE WITH PECANS AND ■ CHEESE ■

INGREDIENTS

■ 1 iceberg lettuce
■ 4oz (125g) curd or ricotta cheese
■ 2 tbsp (30ml) Greek yogurt
■ 1oz (25g) pecan nuts
■ 1oz (25g) sultanas
■ 2oz (50g) fresh redcurrants
■ salt and pepper

Illustrated on page 53

An unusual way of serving lettuce, this makes a surprisingly nutritious meal. If you want to keep the calories low, use a low-fat skimmed-milk soft cheese. If fresh redcurrants are not available, use frozen.

PREPARATION TIME: 20 mins

SERVES 4

METHOD

1 Slice a lid off the top of the iceberg lettuce and cut out the centre, leaving a generous shell (see right). Put the inner part of the lettuce aside.
2 Mix together the curd or ricotta cheese and yogurt in a bowl. Add the pecan nuts, sultanas, and half the redcurrants. Season to taste.
3 Spoon the cheese mixture into the lettuce shell and pack down with a spoon.
4 Garnish with the remaining redcurrants. Shred the inner part of the lettuce and use it as a bed for the filled shell. Refrigerate and when serving use a sharp knife to cut into portions.

MAKING A ■ LETTUCE SHELL ■

*V*egetables can make beautiful decorative cases for a dish. You can either scoop out the centre, mix it with other ingredients as a filling, and then spoon it back into the shell, for example using peppers, tomatoes or courgettes; or you can use the centre as a decoration around the outside of the shell, for example using iceberg lettuce. Both methods enable you to benefit from all the goodness of the vegetable in an economical and attractive way. To ensure the casing is firm, chill the vegetable before filling it.

1 Slice a lid off the top of the iceberg lettuce, using a sharp knife.

2 Cut down inside the lettuce and scoop out the centre, leaving a thick shell to contain a filling.

3 Shred the scooped-out centre of the lettuce and use it as a bed for the stuffed lettuce.

Tabbouleh

◼ TABBOULEH ◼

INGREDIENTS

◼ 6oz (175g) bulgar wheat
◼ pinch salt
◼ ½ pint (300ml) boiling water
◼ ½ cucumber, diced
◼ 4 tbsp (60ml) finely chopped fresh mint
◼ 4 tbsp (60ml) finely chopped fresh parsley

DRESSING
◼ 2–3 tbsp (30–45ml) extra virgin olive oil
◼ 2–3 tbsp (30–45ml) lemon juice
◼ 1 clove garlic, crushed
◼ salt and pepper

Illustrated above

This delicious, satisfying dish is very simple to prepare. The nutty-tasting bulgar wheat provides a strong base for the predominating flavour of fresh herbs. To keep the calorie and fat content low, this recipe has less oil than the traditional version.

PREPARATION TIME: 15 mins (plus 30 mins cooling time)
SERVES 4

METHOD

1 Mix the bulgar wheat with the salt.
2 Pour on the boiling water and leave to cool.
3 Once cold, mix in the cucumber, mint and parsley.
4 Mix together the olive oil, lemon juice and garlic. Season to taste and toss into the salad.

◼ WINTER SLAW ◼

INGREDIENTS

◼ 8oz (250g) carrots, peeled or scrubbed
◼ 4oz (125g) turnip, peeled
◼ 4oz (125g) swede, peeled
◼ 2 tbsp (30ml) tahini
◼ 6 tbsp (90ml) water
◼ 1 tsp (5ml) wholegrain mustard
◼ ½ tsp creamed horseradish
◼ 2 tbsp (30ml) lemon juice
◼ salt and pepper

GARNISH
◼ sprig of coriander

Illustrated below

Root vegetables are high in fibre and full of valuable vitamins and minerals. They are often associated with casseroles and stews, but are delicious raw and when mixed together create an interesting combination of colour and flavour.

PREPARATION TIME: 20 mins
SERVES 4

METHOD

1 Grate the raw vegetables into fine strands and mix together.
2 In a separate bowl, mix the tahini with 2 tbsp (30ml) of the water, beating well until smooth. Add the remaining water gradually.
3 Add the mustard and horseradish to the tahini and stir in the lemon juice. Season to taste.
4 Mix the dressing into the salad and serve immediately.

Winter slaw

Alfalfa salad with marinated mushrooms

ALFALFA SALAD WITH MARINATED ■ MUSHROOMS ■

INGREDIENTS

■ 8oz (250g) cos lettuce leaves
■ 4 tomatoes
■ 2oz (50g) alfalfa sprouts

DRESSING

■ 2 tbsp (30ml) white wine vinegar
■ 4 tbsp (60ml) sunflower oil
■ 2 spring onions, trimmed and finely chopped
■ 1 clove garlic, crushed
■ 1oz (25g) mushrooms, wiped and finely sliced
■ salt and pepper

Illustrated above

Alfalfa sprouts add flavour, texture and extra vitamins and minerals to green salads. Try growing your own from seed (see right); it costs very little and is easy to do.

PREPARATION TIME: 15 mins (plus 2 hours marinating time)
SERVES 4

METHOD

1 Wipe the lettuce leaves, cut the tomatoes into thin wedges and mix carefully with the alfalfa sprouts. Then refrigerate.
2 For the dressing, mix all the ingredients together and leave for 2 hours to marinate. Season to taste.
3 Just before serving the salad, toss in the dressing and serve immediately.

■ SPROUTING BEANS ■

*S*prouting your own beans is cheap and easy, and by using them when they are young and fresh, you can have the full benefit of their high vitamin and mineral content. The following are particularly easy to grow: mung beans, aduki beans, alfalfa, mustard and cress, whole lentils. One handful of seeds will yield about eight handfuls of sprouts. Salad sprouters, which allow you to grow three varieties of seed, are available.

1 Put 2 tbsp (30ml) seeds in a large jam jar and fill it with water. Soak the seeds overnight, then drain away the water.

2 Cover the jar with a piece of muslin, secured with an elastic band and keep in a warm place. Every morning and evening pour lukewarm water through the muslin to rinse the beans, then drain them well.

3 After each rinse, leave the jar upside down to ensure that all the water has drained away. After 2–3 days, put the jar in sunlight for a day or two until the beans are sprouted and continue to rinse with water.

GREEN SALAD WITH RAVIGOTE DRESSING

INGREDIENTS

- 2oz (50g) dried apricots
- 1 punnet salad cress
- 2oz (50g) spinach
- 8oz (250g) crisp lettuce or frisée

DRESSING

- 2 tbsp (30ml) chopped fresh parsley
- 3 spring onions, trimmed and chopped
- ½oz (15g) watercress, finely chopped
- 1 tbsp (15ml) capers
- 2 tbsp (30ml) extra virgin olive oil
- 2 tbsp (30ml) white wine vinegar

Illustrated right

This is a simplified adaptation of the classic French "ravigote" sauce. The ingredients contribute good quantities of essential vitamins and minerals. A little dried fruit adds sweetness and contrast to any leafy salad and, if you like the taste, consider using frisée instead of lettuce for variety.

PREPARATION TIME: 20 mins (plus soaking overnight)

SERVES 4

METHOD

1 Soak the dried apricots overnight. Drain and cut into slivers.
2 Cut and wash the salad cress.
3 Shred the spinach and lettuce (or frisée) into thin strips.
4 Mix all the salad together in a large bowl.
5 For the dressing, mix all the ingredients and toss into the salad just before serving.

CLOCKWISE FROM TOP LEFT: Green salad with ravigote dressing; Mixed leaf salad; Chinese salad with sherry and spice dressing

CHINESE SALAD WITH SHERRY AND SPICE DRESSING

INGREDIENTS

- 2oz (50g) sultanas
- 2 tbsp (30ml) lemon juice
- 10oz (300g) Chinese leaves or spinach
- 4–6 large radishes
- 2oz (50g) bean sprouts (see left)

DRESSING

- 1 tbsp (15ml) lemon juice
- 1 tbsp (15ml) sunflower oil
- 1 tsp (5ml) soya sauce
- 2 tsp (10ml) sherry
- 1 clove garlic, crushed
- ¼ tsp Chinese five-spice powder

Illustrated right

Chinese leaves are highly versatile. They can be used raw in salads or stir-fried, and the stem makes a good, crunchy salad ingredient.

PREPARATION TIME: 45 mins (plus 1–2 hours soaking time)

SERVES 4

METHOD

1 Soak the sultanas in the lemon juice for 1–2 hours.
2 Shred the Chinese leaves or spinach.
3 Slice the radishes thinly and rinse the bean sprouts.
4 Mix the sultanas and all the salad together in a large bowl.
5 For the dressing, mix all the ingredients together and toss into the salad. Serve immediately.

MIXED LEAF SALAD

INGREDIENTS

- 8oz (250g) lamb's lettuce
- 4oz (125g) feuille de chêne or oak leaf lettuce.
- 4oz (125g) sorrel leaves or spinach
- 1 small radicchio – about 4oz (125g)

DRESSING

- 1 tbsp (15ml) extra virgin olive oil
- 2 tbsp (30ml) white wine vinegar
- 3 cloves garlic, finely chopped
- ½ tsp green peppercorns, crushed
- 1 bay leaf
- 2 tsp (10ml) fresh tarragon

Illustrated above

The exotic range of colours, textures and flavours now available in salad leaves have added fresh interest to simple salads. Feuille de chêne, sorrel and radicchio contribute colour, shape and a robust flavour, which offsets the softer, milder lamb's lettuce.

PREPARATION TIME: 25 mins

SERVES 4

METHOD

1 Wipe the lamb's and feuille de chêne lettuces carefully.
2 Shred the sorrel and radicchio into fine strips.
3 Mix all the salad leaves in a large bowl, cover and refrigerate.
4 For the dressing, mix the ingredients together well.
5 Remove the bay leaf. Toss the dressing over the salad just before serving.

■ FLORENCE SALAD ■

INGREDIENTS

■ 2 fennel bulbs
■ 2 pears, preferably William or Packham
■ 2oz (50g) roasted unsalted peanuts
■ 4oz (125g) young spinach leaves

DRESSING

■ 3oz (75g) cottage cheese
■ 1 tbsp (15ml) lemon juice
■ 1 tbsp (15ml) smetana or soured cream
■ 2 tbsp (30ml) mayonnaise (see p.59)
■ ½ tsp celery seeds
■ salt and pepper

Illustrated below

This light, crisp salad has a deliciously rich, creamy dressing. If you want to reduce the calories, use a low-calorie mayonnaise or add only a little dressing to the salad and pass round the rest in a separate bowl.
PREPARATION TIME: 20 mins
SERVES 4

METHOD

1 Trim the fennel bulbs, slice in half and remove the centre layers, leaving a shell for serving the salad. Cut the centre layers into coarse chunks.
2 Core and chop the pears and mix with the fennel chunks and peanuts. Select the best spinach leaves and rinse.
3 For the dressing, mix all the ingredients together in a blender or food processor until completely smooth. Season to taste.
4 Mix the dressing into the salad.
5 Lay the spinach leaves on a large plate, pile the salad into the fennel shell halves and lay them on top of the spinach base.

Red, white and green salad

■ RED, WHITE AND ■ GREEN SALAD ■

INGREDIENTS

■ 1 red pepper, deseeded and diced
■ 4oz (125g) mooli, scrubbed and diced
■ 6oz (175g) mangetout, halved
■ 4oz (125g) Chinese leaves, shredded

DRESSING

■ 1 tbsp (15ml) sesame oil
■ 1 tsp (5ml) soya sauce
■ 1 tsp (5ml) lemon juice
■ ½ tsp honey
■ 1 tsp (5ml) tahini
■ salt and pepper

Illustrated above

This salad is excellent value as very little is wasted in the preparation of all the salad vegetables. Mooli, otherwise known as Daikon, is a large white radish, slightly milder in flavour than the traditional red-skinned variety and with mangetout you eat everything, as the name suggests. The sweet-and-sour dressing brings an appropriately oriental flavour to the Chinese-style salad.
PREPARATION TIME: 25 mins
SERVES 4

METHOD

1 Prepare all the salad ingredients, and place in a salad bowl.
2 For the dressing, mix the ingredients thoroughly together.
3 Pour the dressing over the salad and toss.

Florence salad

■ CLASSIC MAYONNAISE ■

INGREDIENTS

■ 2 egg yolks
■ ½ pint (300ml) mixed olive and sunflower oil
■ 1–2 tbsp (15–30ml) lemon juice or white wine vinegar
■ pinch mustard powder
■ salt and pepper
■ 1 tbsp (15ml) boiling water

A classic mayonnaise can be used as a base for other salad dressings as part of a recipe, or simply as a rich dressing in its own right. It is high in fat, so use sparingly or mix with natural yogurt or low-fat fromage frais. This mayonnaise can be made using dried egg mixture if preferred. It will keep for at least a week in a cool place.

PREPARATION TIME: 15 mins (plus chilling time)
MAKES: ½ pint (300ml)

METHOD

1 Beat the egg yolks thoroughly, in a blender or with a whisk.
2 Add half the oil, a drip at a time, beating continuously.
3 Add 1 tbsp (15ml) lemon juice or vinegar and the mustard powder. Beat well.
4 Add the remaining oil: a tablespoon at a time if whisking by hand; in a steady stream if using an electric whisk. Season.
5 Beat in the boiling water, to stabilize the mayonnaise. Refrigerate and serve chilled.

Hot nut and ginger dressing

■ HOT NUT AND GINGER DRESSING ■

INGREDIENTS

■ 2oz (50g) creamed coconut
■ ½ pint (300ml) boiling water
■ 2 tsp (10ml) sunflower oil
■ 1 small onion, peeled and finely chopped
■ 2 cloves garlic, crushed
■ ¼ tsp chilli powder
■ 4oz (125g) smooth peanut butter
■ ½ inch (1cm) fresh root ginger, grated
■ juice and rind of ½ lemon
■ 2 tsp (10ml) honey
■ soya sauce to taste
■ salt and pepper

Illustrated above

Known as Gado Gado, this is a traditional nut sauce from Indonesia. Serve over a crisp salad or stir-fried vegetables and rice to make a nutritious meal. You could also use it with burgers or baked dishes, but coconut is a rich source of saturated fat, so only serve small portions.

PREPARATION TIME: 10 mins
COOKING TIME: 30 mins
SERVES 4

METHOD

1 Grate the coconut and dissolve it in the boiling water.
2 Heat the oil in a pan and gently fry the onion for 3–4 minutes.
3 Add the remaining ingredients and mix thoroughly. Pour over the coconut milk.
4 Bring to the boil and simmer gently for 30 minutes, stirring frequently. Season to taste.

■ FRENCH DRESSING ■

INGREDIENTS

■ 1 tbsp (15ml) white wine vinegar
■ 4 tbsp (60ml) extra virgin olive oil
■ 2 spring onions, trimmed and finely chopped
■ 1–2 cloves garlic, crushed
■ salt and pepper

Illustrated on page 60

A versatile oil and vinegar dressing has countless possibilities for variations with herbs and spices. This is a slightly lighter and sharper version of a recipe much favoured on the Continent of 1 part vinegar to 6 parts oil, but it is still milder than the traditional 1 to 3 ratio.

PREPARATION TIME: 10 mins
MAKES: 3fl oz (75ml)

METHOD

1 Mix together all the ingredients very thoroughly. Season to taste, and store in a screw-top jar in the fridge.
2 Shake vigorously before using. If you make larger quantities, it will keep for at least 2 weeks if refrigerated.

PEANUT AND
■ TOMATO DRESSING ■

INGREDIENTS

■ 1 oz (25g) salted
peanuts
■ 2 tomatoes,
skinned and
chopped
■ 1 tsp (5ml) tomato
purée
■ 2–3 tbsp (10–15ml)
lemon juice
■ 3 tbsp (45ml)
groundnut oil
■ pinch chilli powder
■ salt and pepper

Illustrated right

This tangy, colourful dressing adds
interest to the simplest green salad and
contributes a healthy quantity of protein
and Vitamin C.
PREPARATION TIME: 15 mins
MAKES: 7fl oz (200ml)

METHOD

1 In a food processor, grind the peanuts
into fine pieces.
2 Add the tomatoes, tomato purée and
lemon juice and blend thoroughly.
3 Gradually drip in the oil, blending
continuously, until the mixture is thick and
creamy.
4 Add the chilli powder and season to
taste.

■ CHINESE DRESSING ■

INGREDIENTS

■ ½ green chilli
■ 1 clove garlic
■ 1 tbsp (15ml)
sunflower oil
■ 1 tsp (5ml) sesame
oil
■ 1 tbsp (15ml) cider
vinegar
■ 1 tsp (5ml) soya
sauce
■ 1 tsp (5ml) sherry
■ salt and pepper

Illustrated right

This sharp, spicy dressing mixes well with
strong-flavoured vegetables, bean sprouts
and tofu (bean curd).
PREPARATION TIME: 15 mins
MAKES: 2fl oz (60ml)

METHOD

1 Deseed and dice the chilli. Crush the
garlic.
2 Mix all the ingredients together, stirring
thoroughly.
3 Store in a screw-top jar in the fridge and
shake well before using. If you make larger
quantities, it will keep for about 2 weeks.

*CLOCKWISE FROM TOP LEFT: Peanut and tomato dressing; Walnut dressing;
Chinese dressing; French dressing (see p.59)*

■ WALNUT DRESSING ■

INGREDIENTS

- ■ 4oz (125g) walnut pieces
- ■ 2 cloves garlic
- ■ ½–1 tsp (2–5ml) green peppercorns
- ■ 1 tsp (5ml) soya sauce
- ■ 2 tbsp (30ml) extra virgin olive oil
- ■ 2 tbsp (30ml) lemon juice
- ■ 2fl oz–¼ pint (50–150ml) water

Illustrated left

This substantial dressing goes well with chunky salads, bean sprouts or savoury rissoles. To prevent the mixture curdling, add the water very slowly while you blend. This allows it to emulsify with the oils in the nuts without separating.

PREPARATION TIME: 10 mins
MAKES: ½ pint (300ml)

METHOD

1 In a food processor, grind the walnuts with the garlic and peppercorns.
2 Add the soya sauce, olive oil and lemon juice and blend.
3 Add the water very gradually, blending continuously, until the dressing has the consistency of thick yogurt.

■ FRESH TOMATO RELISH ■

INGREDIENTS

- ■ 3oz (75g) dried stoned dates
- ■ 4oz (125g) dried apple rings
- ■ 1 small onion, peeled and finely chopped
- ■ 2–3 tbsp (30–45ml) red wine vinegar
- ■ 3 tomatoes, skinned and chopped
- ■ 2 tbsp (30ml) tomato purée
- ■ ½ inch (1cm) fresh root ginger, peeled and grated
- ■ ½ tsp allspice
- ■ ½ tsp mustard seeds
- ■ salt and pepper

Illustrated right

Home-made relishes lend spice and moisture to nut and seed snacks and to chunky vegetable salads. They are easy to prepare and can be sugar-, salt- and additive-free.

PREPARATION TIME: 30 mins
SERVES 4

METHOD

1 Finely chop or mince the dates and apple rings.
2 Mix with the onion.
3 In a blender or food processor, mix the vinegar, tomatoes and tomato purée together until smooth.
4 Mix the tomato sauce with the fruit mixture and add the spices and seasoning to taste.
5 Keep in the fridge and use within 5–6 days.

FROM LEFT: Tahini and apricot relish; Fresh tomato relish

■ TAHINI AND APRICOT RELISH ■

INGREDIENTS

- ■ 2oz (50g) dried apricots, soaked
- ■ 1 onion, peeled and chopped
- ■ 1 small green pepper, deseeded and chopped
- ■ ½ green chilli, deseeded and diced
- ■ 2 tbsp (30ml) cider vinegar
- ■ 1 tsp (5ml) tahini
- ■ salt and pepper

Illustrated above

Quick to prepare and free from refined sugar, additives and preservatives, this relish makes a tasty accompaniment to savoury rissoles and loaves or use it as a chunky salad dressing.

PREPARATION TIME: 10 mins (plus overnight soaking time)
SERVES 4

METHOD

1 Drain the apricots and slice finely.
2 Prepare the onion, pepper and chilli and mix with the apricots.
3 Add the vinegar, then mix in the tahini. Season to taste.
4 Serve immediately.

PASTA AND PANCAKES

CLOCKWISE FROM TOP: Yeasted pancakes with soured cream and olives (see p.66); Cornmeal pancakes with sweet potato filling (see p.65); Buckwheat pancakes with bean sprouts, mushrooms and water chestnuts (see p.66); Chilli cornmeal pancakes (see p.66)

WHOLEMEAL BATTER

INGREDIENTS

- 1 egg
- ½ pint (300ml) skimmed milk
- 1 tsp (5ml) sunflower oil
- 4oz (125g) plain wholemeal flour
- oil for frying

Wholemeal flour can be used to make excellent pancakes, and with a little practice you can make them light and lacy. Make sure the mixture is well beaten.

PREPARATION TIME: 5 mins (plus 30 mins resting time)

COOKING TIME: 30 mins

MAKES: 8–10 pancakes

METHOD

1 Liquidize the egg, milk and oil in a blender or food processor for 30 seconds. Add the flour and liquidize for 30 seconds.
2 Heat a 7 inch (18cm) pancake pan. Put in a little oil and wipe over with absorbent kitchen paper. Pour in 2 tbsp (30ml) batter and cook for 2 minutes until the top has set. Loosen the edges of the pancake with a spatula. Cook the other side for 1 minute.

BUCKWHEAT BATTER

INGREDIENTS

- ½ pint (300ml) milk
- 1 tsp (5ml) sunflower oil
- 1 egg
- 2oz (50g) plain wholemeal flour
- 2oz (50g) buckwheat flour
- pinch of salt
- oil for frying

A buckwheat batter has a darker appearance and more tangy flavour than a wholemeal one. The best results come from mixing the two flours together.

PREPARATION TIME: 5 mins (plus 30 mins resting time)

COOKING TIME: 30 mins

MAKES: 8–10 pancakes

METHOD

1 Mix the milk, oil and egg together in a blender or food processor for 30 seconds. Add the flours and salt and blend again until a smooth batter forms. Allow the mixture to stand for 30 minutes.
2 Heat a little oil in a 7 inch (18cm) pancake pan. Pour in 2–3 tbsp (30–45ml) of batter and cook for 2 minutes until the top has set. Loosen the edges of the pancake with a spatula. Cook the other side for 1 minute.

MAKING PANCAKES

*P*ancakes are easy and fun to make. The batter can be prepared a day in advance or, since pancakes freeze well, you could make a large batch and defrost them as required. Buckwheat and wholemeal flour make nutritious batter, but experiment with different flours for interesting flavours and textures (see left).

1 Heat a little oil in a pan, then pour in 2–3 tbsp (30–45ml) of batter.

2 Tilt the pan until the batter has spread out evenly. Fry for 2–3 minutes.

3 Toss or turn the pancake with a wooden spatula and cook for 2–3 minutes on the other side.

❚ YEASTED BATTER ❚

INGREDIENTS

- ¼oz (10g) fresh yeast (or ½ tsp dried yeast)
- 6 tbsp (90ml) lukewarm water
- 1 egg, separated
- 2oz (50g) plain wholemeal flour
- 2oz (50g) buckwheat flour
- ¼ tsp oil for frying

These tasty pancakes are well worth the extra effort.

PREPARATION TIME: 1½ hours
COOKING TIME: 10 mins
MAKES: 8–10 pancakes

METHOD

1 Put the fresh yeast in a small bowl and gradually mix in the warm water (sprinkle dried yeast with water and leave for 5 minutes). Beat in the egg yolk.
2 Mix the flours together in a bowl. Beat in the yeast mixture. Cover with clingfilm or a damp cloth and leave for 1 hour until the batter has doubled in bulk.
3 Whisk the egg white until firm. Beat the batter with a spoon to knock it back. Stir in 1 tbsp (15ml) egg white, then fold in the rest. Cover and leave to rest for 20 minutes.
4 Heat a griddle or heavy-based frying pan over a medium heat. Pour in the oil and wipe over with absorbent kitchen paper. Use about 1 tbsp (15ml) of batter for each pancake. Fry 3 or 4 at a time, on a medium heat for 2 minutes on each side.

❚ CORNMEAL BATTER ❚

INGREDIENTS

- 9fl oz (275ml) water
- 1oz (25g) margarine or butter
- 3oz (75g) cornmeal
- 4oz (125g) plain wholemeal flour

Cornmeal is a coarse yellow flour also called maize meal.

PREPARATION TIME: 30 mins
COOKING TIME: 30 mins
MAKES: 8 pancakes

METHOD

1 Put the water in a saucepan with half the margarine. Bring to the boil. Reduce the heat, add the cornmeal and stir quickly. Cover and cook very gently for 5 minutes. Leave to cool.
2 Combine the wholemeal flour and the cornmeal mixture in a mixing bowl. Knead to form a soft dough. Divide into eight pieces. Dust a work surface with cornmeal and roll out each piece into a 7 inch (18cm) circle.
3 Cook on a hot, ungreased griddle or frying pan for 1–2 minutes on each side.

❚ CORNMEAL PANCAKES WITH ❚ ❚ SWEET POTATO FILLING ❚

INGREDIENTS

- 1 sweet potato (about 1lb/500g in weight)
- 2 tsp (10ml) sunflower oil
- 1 onion, finely chopped
- 1 yellow pepper, deseeded and chopped
- ½ tsp ground mace
- 1½oz (40g) creamed coconut, grated
- salt and pepper
- 1 quantity of cornmeal batter (see left)

Illustrated on page 63

Creamed coconut makes a delicious addition to these pancakes, but it is important to weigh the amount carefully, as coconut has a very high fat content.

PREPARATION TIME: 45 mins (plus 30 mins for the batter)
COOKING TIME: 30 mins (plus 30 minutes for the pancakes)
MAKES: 8 pancakes

METHOD

1 Boil the sweet potato for 20 minutes. Drain, reserving the stock. Peel the potato and mash the flesh.
2 Meanwhile, heat the oil and fry the onion and pepper for 5 minutes until soft. Add the mace and cook slowly for a further 3 minutes, stirring occasionally.
3 Make a coconut milk by blending the coconut with 4 tbsp (60ml) hot sweet potato stock. Add the onion, pepper and mashed sweet potato. Season to taste. Cover and keep warm.
4 Make the pancakes (see opposite). Put 2 tbsp (30ml) of filling in the centre of each pancake and serve.

BUCKWHEAT PANCAKES WITH BEAN SPROUTS, MUSHROOMS AND ■ WATER CHESTNUTS ■

INGREDIENTS

■ 1 quantity of buckwheat batter (see p.64)
■ 2 tsp (10ml) sesame oil
■ 2oz (50g) blanched almonds
■ 6 spring onions, sliced
■ 1 clove garlic, crushed
■ 4oz (125g) bean sprouts
■ 4oz (125g) button mushrooms, chopped
■ 4oz (125g) canned water chestnuts
■ 1 tsp (5ml) arrowroot or cornflour
■ 2 tbsp (30ml) soya sauce
■ 2 tsp (10ml) clear honey
■ 4 tbsp (60ml) medium sherry
■ 1 tsp (5ml) grated fresh root ginger
■ 1 tbsp (15ml) lemon juice

Illustrated on page 63

Bean sprouts have a valuable protein and vitamin content.
PREPARATION TIME: 25 mins (plus 30 mins for the batter)
COOKING TIME: 15 mins (plus 30 mins for the pancakes)
MAKES: 8–10 pancakes

METHOD

1 Make the pancakes (see p.64)
2 For the filling, heat the oil and fry the almonds until they are lightly browned. Add the spring onions, garlic, bean sprouts, mushrooms and water chestnuts. Fry gently for 5 minutes, stirring occasionally.
3 For the sauce, put the arrowroot or cornflour in a saucepan. Gradually stir in the soya sauce. Add the honey, sherry, ginger and lemon juice. Boil, stirring constantly. Remove from the heat and season.
4 Stir half of the sauce into the filling. Put 2 tbsp (30ml) of filling into each pancake and roll up. Arrange on an ovenproof dish and cover with foil. Heat through in a preheated oven at Gas Mark 4, 350°F, 180°C for 15 minutes. Reheat the remaining sauce and pour over the pancakes.

CHILLI CORNMEAL ■ PANCAKES ■

INGREDIENTS

■ 8oz (250g) red kidney beans, soaked, or a 15oz (430g) can, drained
■ 2 tbsp (30ml) corn oil
■ 1 onion, finely chopped
■ 1 red pepper, deseeded and chopped
■ 2 cloves garlic, crushed
■ ¼ tsp chilli powder
■ 2 tbsp (30ml) tomato purée
■ salt and pepper
■ 1 quantity of cornmeal batter (see p.65)

Illustrated on page 63

The red beans and chilli powder give a truly Mexican flavour to these pancakes. If using canned beans, omit step 1.
PREPARATION TIME: 10 mins (plus 10-12 hours soaking time and 30 mins for the batter)
COOKING TIME: 15 mins (plus 1 hour for the beans and 30 mins for the pancakes)
MAKES: 8 pancakes

METHOD

1 Drain the beans and place in a saucepan with plenty of fresh water. Boil fast for 10 minutes, then simmer for 50 minutes.
2 Drain the beans, mash and set aside.
3 Heat the oil and fry the onion, pepper and garlic for 5 minutes. Add the chilli powder and cook for 2 minutes, stirring constantly. Add the mashed beans and tomato purée. Heat through, stirring occasionally. Season.
4 Meanwhile, make the pancakes (see p.64). Put about 2 tbsp (30ml) filling in the centre of each and serve.

YEASTED PANCAKES WITH SOURED CREAM AND ■ OLIVES ■

INGREDIENTS

■ ½ pint (300ml) soured cream or smetana
■ 16 stoned green olives, chopped
■ 4 small gherkins, diced
■ 2 tbsp (30ml) chopped fresh chives
■ salt and pepper
■ 1 quantity of yeasted batter (see p.65)

Illustrated on page 63

The buckwheat flour in these pancakes gives them a wonderful flavour. The yeast gives them a light texture, and they are well worth the extra effort required to make them.
PREPARATION TIME: 5 mins (plus 1½ hours for the batter)
COOKING TIME: 10 mins
MAKES: about 8 pancakes

METHOD

1 For the sauce, put the soured cream in a small bowl. Stir in the olives, gherkins and chopped chives. Season to taste.
2 Make the yeasted pancakes (see p.64). Serve hot on individual plates, accompanied by spoonfuls of the sauce.

FROM LEFT: Barley and hazelnut pancakes; Beetroot and red bean pancakes

BARLEY AND HAZELNUT
■ PANCAKES ■

INGREDIENTS

■ 2oz (50g) pearl barley
■ 1 quantity of wholemeal batter (see p.64)
■ 2 tsp (10ml) hazelnut oil
■ 1oz (25g) hazelnuts, coarsely chopped
■ 2 onions, finely chopped
■ 1 clove garlic, crushed
■ 2oz (50g) carrots, finely diced
■ 1 tsp (5ml) chopped fresh thyme
■ 6 tbsp (90ml) buttermilk or ordinary milk
■ 7oz (200g) can of chopped tomatoes
■ salt and pepper

Illustrated above

Pearl barley makes a chewy and substantial filling for pancakes. Here it is mixed with crunchy hazelnuts and creamy buttermilk to give a good mixture of textures.

PREPARATION TIME: 50 mins (plus 50 mins for the barley and 30 mins for the batter)
COOKING TIME: 40 mins
MAKES: 8–10 pancakes

METHOD

1 For the filling, boil the barley for 50 minutes until the barley is tender, drain. Make the pancakes (see p.64). Heat the oil and fry the hazelnuts for 3 minutes. Add half the chopped onions and the garlic. Fry for 5 minutes. Add the carrots and thyme and cook for a further 5 minutes, stirring. Allow to cool then stir in the buttermilk and the barley.
2 Put 2 tbsp (30ml) of filling into each pancake and roll up. Arrange on an ovenproof dish and cover with foil. Heat in a preheated oven at Gas Mark 4, 350°F, 180°C for 10 minutes.
3 Gently fry the remaining onion for 5 minutes. Add the tomatoes, boil, then simmer for 10 minutes. Purée the sauce, add seasoning, then pour over the pancakes and serve.

BEETROOT AND
■ RED BEAN PANCAKES ■

INGREDIENTS

■ 2oz (50g) aduki beans, soaked, or 7oz (200g) canned red kidney beans, drained
■ 8oz (250g) raw beetroot
■ 1 quantity of wholemeal batter (see p.64)
■ 1 tbsp (15ml) lemon juice
■ 1 tsp (5ml) arrowroot or cornflour
■ 6 spring onions, sliced
■ ¼ pint (150ml) smetana or soured cream
■ 1 tbsp (15ml) chopped fresh chives
■ salt and pepper

Illustrated left

Aduki beans and beetroot give a sweetish filling with a nutty texture. However, if you don't want to soak and cook the aduki beans, this pancake filling could be equally good made with a can of red kidney beans.

PREPARATION TIME: 55 mins (plus 10–12 hours soaking time and 30 mins for the batter)
COOKING TIME: 45 mins (plus 45 mins for the beans)
MAKES: 8–10 pancakes

METHOD

1 For the filling, boil the beans fast for 10 minutes, then simmer for 35 minutes. Drain well, reserving ½ pint (300ml) of the liquid. Peel and dice the beetroot and simmer in the reserved stock for 20–25 minutes. Make the pancakes (see p.64).
2 Mix the arrowroot or cornflour with the lemon juice and add to the beetroot. Boil, stirring all the time. Remove from heat, add the onions and season.
3 Put 2 tbsp (30ml) of filling into each pancake and roll up. Arrange on an ovenproof dish and cover with foil. Heat in a preheated oven at Gas Mark 4, 350°F, 180°C for 15 minutes and serve garnished with smetana or soured cream and chopped chives.

BUCKWHEAT PANCAKES WITH GINGER, LEEK AND ■ MUSHROOM ■

INGREDIENTS

- 1 tbsp (15ml) sunflower oil
- 1 onion, finely chopped
- 1 clove garlic, crushed
- ½ tsp ground coriander seeds
- 1 tbsp (15ml) grated fresh root ginger
- 4oz (125g) leeks, sliced
- 4oz (125g) button mushrooms, sliced
- 7oz (200g) can of chopped tomatoes
- salt and pepper
- 1 quantity of buckwheat batter (see p.64)
- ¼ pint (150ml) buttermilk or ordinary milk
- 1 tbsp (15ml) chopped fresh chives

Illustrated right

Buttermilk, yogurt and smetana make low-fat garnishes for pancakes. Fresh herbs enhance the appearance.

PREPARATION TIME: 30 mins (plus 30 mins for the batter)

COOKING TIME: 15 mins (plus 30 mins for the pancakes)

MAKES: 8–10 pancakes

METHOD

1 For the filling, fry the onion and garlic in the oil for 5 minutes. Add the coriander, ginger, leeks and mushrooms and cook gently for a further 5 minutes. Add the tomatoes. Boil, then simmer for 10 minutes. Season to taste.

2 Meanwhile, make the pancakes (see p.64). Put 2 tbsp (30ml) of filling on to each and roll up. Arrange on an ovenproof dish. Cover with foil and heat in a preheated oven at Gas Mark 4, 350°F, 180°C for 15 minutes.

3 Mix the buttermilk (or yogurt) and chopped chives. Spoon on to the pancakes and serve.

BUCKWHEAT PANCAKES WITH ASPARAGUS AND ■ COTTAGE CHEESE ■

INGREDIENTS

- 1 quantity of buckwheat batter (see p.64)
- 8oz (250g) fresh asparagus spears, trimmed
- 1 egg, beaten
- 12oz (375g) cottage cheese or cream cheese
- 2 tsp (10ml) lemon juice
- 1 tbsp (15ml) sunflower oil
- 1 tbsp (15ml) mayonnaise
- 2 tbsp (30ml) natural yogurt

Illustrated above

Half-fat cottage cheese and low-calorie mayonnaise would reduce the fat content of this recipe.

PREPARATION TIME: 20 mins (plus 30 mins for the batter)

COOKING TIME: 20 mins (plus 30 mins for the pancakes)

MAKES: 8–10 pancakes

METHOD

1 Make the pancakes (see p.64). For the filling, steam the asparagus spears for 5 minutes. Cut into short lengths. Mix the egg and 8oz (250g) cottage cheese. Stir in the spears.

2 Put about 2 tbsp (30ml) filling on to each pancake and roll up. Arrange on a greased ovenproof dish. Cover with foil and bake in a preheated oven at Gas Mark 4, 350°F, 180°C for 20 minutes.

3 For the sauce, liquidise the remaining cottage cheese, lemon juice, oil, mayonnaise and yogurt, until smooth. Pour over the pancakes and serve.

FROM LEFT: Spinach buckwheat pancakes; Buckwheat pancakes with ginger, leek and mushroom; Ratatouille buckwheat pancakes; Buckwheat pancakes with asparagus and cottage cheese

SPINACH BUCKWHEAT PANCAKES ▮

INGREDIENTS

- 1 quantity of buckwheat batter (see p.64)
- 1½lb (750g) fresh spinach (or 8oz/250g frozen spinach)
- 1oz (25g) pine kernels
- 1oz (25g) raisins
- 6 tbsp (90ml) buttermilk or ordinary milk
- ½ tsp ground nutmeg
- 1 tsp (5ml) extra virgin olive oil
- 1oz (25g) grated Parmesan cheese

Illustrated above

The spinach, pine kernels and raisins give a varied flavour and texture.

PREPARATION TIME: 25 mins (plus 30 mins for the batter)

COOKING TIME: 15 mins (plus 30 mins for the pancakes)

MAKES: 8–10 pancakes

METHOD

1 Make the pancakes (see p.64). For the filling, wash the fresh spinach and put in a pan without any extra liquid. Cook for 5 minutes (cook frozen spinach as instructed on packet). Purée the spinach with the pine kernels, raisins, buttermilk and nutmeg. Spread 2 tbsp (30ml) of filling over each pancake, then fold in half and in half again to give a fan shape.

2 Arrange on a greased ovenproof dish. Brush with oil and sprinkle with Parmesan. Cover with foil and heat through in a preheated oven at Gas Mark 4, 350°F, 180°C for 15 minutes.

RATATOUILLE BUCKWHEAT ▮ PANCAKES ▮

INGREDIENTS

- 1–2 tbsp (15–30ml) olive oil
- 1 onion, sliced into rings
- 1 clove garlic, crushed
- 1 aubergine, cut into cubes
- 8oz (250g) courgettes, sliced
- 8oz (250g) tomatoes, chopped
- 3 tbsp (45ml) tomato purée
- 1 tbsp (15ml) chopped fresh parsley
- 2 tsp (10ml) chopped fresh thyme
- 1 bay leaf
- salt and pepper
- 1 quantity of buckwheat batter (see p.64)
- ¼ pint (150ml) natural yogurt or soured cream
- 1 tbsp (15ml) chopped fresh parsley

Illustrated left

Aubergine, courgettes and tomatoes combine well in this classic ratatouille filling to make a well-balanced dish that is low in fat.

PREPARATION TIME: 40 mins (plus 30 mins for the batter)

COOKING TIME: 15 mins (plus 30 mins for the pancakes)

MAKES: 8–10 pancakes

METHOD

1 For the filling, fry the onion and garlic in the oil for 5 minutes. Add the aubergine and courgettes and fry for 5 minutes more, stirring occasionally. Add the tomatoes, tomato purée, parsley, thyme and bay leaf. Boil, then cover and simmer for 15 minutes. Season to taste.

2 Meanwhile, make the pancakes (see p.64). Put 2 tbsp (30ml) of filling on to each pancake and roll up. Arrange on an ovenproof dish. Cover with foil and heat through in a preheated oven at Gas Mark 4, 350°F, 180°C for 15 minutes.

3 Serve with the yogurt and parsley spooned on top.

BASIL AND WALNUT
■ TAGLIATELLE ■

INGREDIENTS

- ■ 12oz (375g) wholemeal tagliatelle
- ■ 5 pints (3 litres) water
- ■ 1 tsp (5ml) lemon juice
- ■ 1oz (25g) chopped fresh basil
- ■ 1oz (25g) pine kernels
- ■ 1oz (25g) walnut halves
- ■ 1oz (25g) grated Parmesan cheese
- ■ 1 clove garlic, crushed
- ■ 4 tbsp (60ml) extra virgin olive oil
- ■ salt and pepper

Illustrated right

This is a version of the famous Italian pesto sauce. It is essential to use fresh basil, as the dried herb does not have the right colour or consistency.

PREPARATION TIME: 5 mins
COOKING TIME: 10 mins
SERVES 4

METHOD

1 Cook the tagliatelle by simmering in the water with the lemon juice, for 8 minutes (4 minutes for fresh pasta).
2 For the sauce, put the basil, pine kernels, walnuts, Parmesan and garlic into a blender or food processor. Purée for about 30 seconds. With the blender or processor on, gradually add the oil and blend until smooth. Season to taste.
3 Drain the pasta. Serve each portion with 1 tbsp (15ml) of sauce.

MUSHROOM TAGLIATELLE WITH VERMOUTH AND ■ TARRAGON ■

INGREDIENTS

- ■ 1 tbsp (15ml) virgin olive oil
- ■ 12oz (375g) button mushrooms, sliced
- ■ 2 cloves garlic, crushed
- ■ 2 tbsp (30ml) dry vermouth
- ■ 4 tsp (20ml) chopped fresh tarragon
- ■ 12oz (375g) wholemeal tagliatelle
- ■ 5 pints (3 litres) water
- ■ 1 tsp (5ml) lemon juice
- ■ salt and pepper

Illustrated right

Dry vermouth is a fortified wine which is flavoured with several herbs and combines well with the tarragon in this dish.

PREPARATION TIME: 5 mins
COOKING TIME: 10 mins (plus 8 mins for the pasta)
SERVES 4

METHOD

1 For the sauce, heat the oil in a pan and fry the mushrooms and garlic for 5 minutes until the juices run. Add the dry vermouth and tarragon. Cover the pan and simmer for 10 minutes.
2 Meanwhile, cook the tagliatelle by simmering in the water with the lemon juice, for 8 minutes (3–4 minutes for fresh pasta). Drain well. Mix with the sauce, season to taste and serve immediately.

FROM LEFT: Mushroom tagliatelle with vermouth and tarragon; Basil and walnut tagliatelle

■ FLAGEOLET NEAPOLITAN ■

INGREDIENTS

- ■ 6oz (175g) flageolet beans, soaked, or a 15oz (430g) can, drained
- ■ 1 tbsp (15ml) olive oil
- ■ 1 onion, peeled and finely chopped
- ■ 1–2 cloves garlic, crushed
- ■ 14oz (400g) can tomatoes
- ■ 1 tbsp (15ml) fresh basil
- ■ 1 bay leaf
- ■ 1 tbsp (15ml) capers
- ■ 2oz (50g) green olives
- ■ salt and pepper
- ■ 8–12oz (250–375g) wholemeal spaghetti or tagliatelle
- ■ 5 pints (3 litres) water, containing 1 tsp (5ml) lemon juice

GARNISH

- ■ Parmesan cheese, grated

Illustrated right

Beans and pasta provide a high-fibre, high-protein meal. If using canned beans, follow the recipe from step 2.

PREPARATION TIME: 40 mins (plus 10–12 hours soaking time)
COOKING TIME: 40 mins (plus 40 mins for the beans)
SERVES 4

METHOD

1 Drain the beans. Place in a pan with plenty of fresh water, bring to the boil and boil fast for 10 minutes, then cover and simmer for 20–30 minutes or until soft. Drain.
2 Heat the oil in a pan and gently fry the onion for 3–4 minutes. Add the garlic and cooked beans and fry for a further 3–4 minutes, stirring well.
3 Add the tomatoes, basil, bay leaf, capers and olives and bring to the boil. Reduce the heat and simmer, uncovered, for 30 minutes. Season to taste.
4 When the sauce is nearly ready to serve, cook the pasta by simmering it in the boiling water for 8–12 minutes or until just tender (3–4 minutes for fresh pasta). Drain.
5 Serve the pasta topped with flageolet sauce, and hand round the Parmesan cheese separately.

PECAN PASTA WITH OYSTER ■ MUSHROOMS ■

INGREDIENTS

- 1 tbsp (15ml) olive oil
- 1 onion, peeled and finely chopped
- 1 clove garlic, crushed
- 4oz (125g) pecan nuts
- 8oz (250g) oyster mushrooms, halved
- 6 artichoke bottoms, halved
- 14oz (400g) can tomatoes
- 2 tbsp (30ml) tomato purée
- 2 tbsp (30ml) red wine vinegar
- 3 tbsp (45ml) finely chopped fresh parsley
- 2 tsp (10ml) dried oregano
- 2 tsp (10ml) capers, chopped
- 2oz (50g) black or green olives, stoned
- pinch chilli powder
- salt and pepper
- 1lb (500g) wholemeal tagliatelle

Illustrated right

Pecan nuts and oyster mushrooms add a delicate flavour to this tomato sauce. The mushrooms resemble oyster shells – hence the name – and can only be eaten when young, as their flesh soon becomes rather hard. They also take longer to soften during cooking than ordinary mushrooms. Pecan nuts resemble walnuts when shelled, although the pecan shell is much smoother and glossier than the furrowed walnut shell. The name pecan comes from an 18th century word meaning "difficult to crack", although in fact they are much easier to crack than almonds, Brazil nuts or walnuts. Like most nuts, pecans are a good source of protein and contain potassium, phosphorus and some B Vitamins. They are excellent in both sweet and savoury dishes.

PREPARATION TIME: 20 mins
COOKING TIME: 35 mins
SERVES 4

METHOD

1 Heat the oil in a pan and gently fry the onion until soft and translucent.
2 Add the garlic and pecan nuts and cook for 3–4 minutes or until the nuts are lightly toasted.
3 Add the mushrooms and artichoke bottoms and cook for 3 minutes.
4 Add all the remaining ingredients except the tagliatelle, bring the sauce to the boil and simmer, uncovered, for 15–20 minutes. Season well.
5 Meanwhile, place the tagliatelle in a large pan of boiling, salted water and cook for 8–10 minutes, or until just tender (3–4 minutes for fresh pasta). Drain well.
6 Serve topped with the pecan and mushroom sauce.

FROM TOP: Flageolet Neapolitan; Pecan pasta with oyster mushrooms

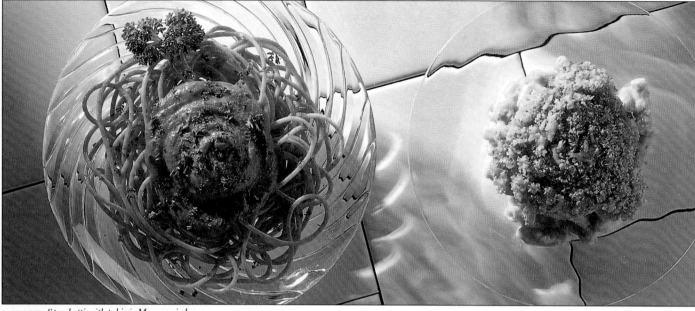

FROM LEFT: Spaghetti with tahini; Macaroni cheese

SPAGHETTI WITH
■ TAHINI ■

Tahini, or sesame seed paste, is a rich food. It is a good idea to dilute it before use, either with water or, as here, with wine and orange juice.

PREPARATION TIME: 5 mins
COOKING TIME: 12 mins
SERVES 4

INGREDIENTS

■ 12oz (375g) wholemeal spaghetti
■ 5 pints (3 litres) water
■ 1 tsp (5ml) lemon juice
■ 2 tbsp (30ml) light tahini
■ 1 clove garlic, crushed
■ 2 tbsp (30ml) tomato purée
■ 2 tbsp (30ml) red wine
■ 6 tbsp (90ml) orange juice

GARNISH
■ 2 tbsp (30ml) chopped fresh parsley

Illustrated above

METHOD

1 Cook the spaghetti by simmering in the water with the lemon juice, for 10–12 minutes (3–4 minutes for fresh pasta).
2 Meanwhile, in a small bowl, mix the tahini with the garlic and the tomato purée. Add the red wine and orange juice and mix until it forms a smooth creamy consistency.
3 When the spaghetti is cooked, drain it well. Serve with the sauce spooned on top and garnish with the chopped parsley.

■ MACARONI CHEESE ■

A favourite with adults and children.
PREPARATION TIME: 15 mins
COOKING TIME: 20 mins (plus 10 mins for the pasta)
SERVES 4

INGREDIENTS

■ 12oz (375g) wholemeal macaroni
■ 5 pints (3 litres) water
■ 1 tsp (5ml) lemon juice
■ 1½oz (40g) margarine or butter
■ 1¼oz (35g) plain wholemeal flour
■ 1 tsp (5ml) mustard powder
■ 1½ pints (900ml) milk
■ salt and pepper
■ 4oz (125g) Cheddar cheese, grated
■ 2oz (50g) fresh wholemeal breadcrumbs

Illustrated above

METHOD

1 Cook the macaroni by simmering in the water and lemon juice, for 10 minutes.
2 For the sauce, melt the margarine in a saucepan. Add the flour, stir rapidly, then cook over a medium heat for 3 minutes until the roux is light and frothy. Stir in the mustard. Gradually add the milk. Bring to the boil, stirring all the time. Stir in half the grated cheese and cook briefly to melt it. Simmer for 5 minutes. Season to taste.
3 When the macaroni is cooked, drain well and combine with the sauce. Put into a greased ovenproof dish. Mix the remaining grated cheese with the breadcrumbs and sprinkle over the top. Bake in a preheated oven at Gas Mark 6, 400°F, 200°C for 20 minutes until the top is bubbling and browned.

MACARONI WITH CHICK
∎ PEAS AND TOMATOES ∎

INGREDIENTS

- ∎ 6oz (175g) dried chick peas, soaked, or a 15oz (430g) can, drained
- ∎ 1 tbsp (15ml) olive oil
- ∎ 2 onions, peeled and roughly chopped
- ∎ 1–2 cloves garlic, crushed
- ∎ ½ tsp caraway seeds
- ∎ 8oz (250g) tomatoes, skinned and chopped
- ∎ 12oz (375g) wholemeal macaroni
- ∎ 5 pints (3 litres) water
- ∎ 4 tsp (20ml) lemon juice
- ∎ salt and pepper

Illustrated right

Chick peas have an attractive and very distinctive flavour, and the added advantage that they can be overcooked without going mushy. Like other pulses, they are extremely nutritious – here they combine with the wholemeal in the macaroni to make a dish particularly high in protein. If using canned chick peas, follow the recipe from step 2.

PREPARATION TIME: 10 mins (plus 10–12 hours soaking time)

COOKING TIME: 15–20 mins (plus 1 ½ hours for the beans and 10 mins for the pasta)

SERVES 4

METHOD

1 For the sauce, drain the chick peas, put into a large saucepan with plenty of fresh water. Bring to the boil and boil fast for 10 minutes, then reduce the heat and simmer for a further 50–80 minutes until the chick peas are tender. Drain well.

2 Heat the oil in a medium-sized saucepan and gently fry the onion and garlic for 5 minutes until the onion is soft but not browned.

3 Add the chick peas, caraway seeds and tomatoes. Bring to the boil. Reduce the heat, cover and simmer for 15 minutes, stirring occasionally until the sauce thickens slightly.

4 Meanwhile, cook the macaroni by simmering in the water with 1 tsp (5ml) lemon juice, for 10 minutes.

5 When the macaroni is cooked, drain well. Add the remaining lemon juice to the sauce with salt and pepper to taste. Stir the sauce into the macaroni and serve.

FROM LEFT: Macaroni with chick peas and tomatoes; Macaroni with oyster mushrooms

MACARONI WITH OYSTER
∎ MUSHROOMS ∎

INGREDIENTS

- ∎ 1½oz (40g) margarine or butter
- ∎ 1¼oz (35g) plain wholemeal flour
- ∎ 1 pint (600ml) skimmed milk
- ∎ 8oz (250g) oyster mushrooms
- ∎ 1 tsp (5ml) chopped fresh dill weed
- ∎ 12oz (375g) wholemeal macaroni
- ∎ 5 pints (3 litres) water
- ∎ 1 tsp (5ml) lemon juice
- ∎ salt and pepper

Illustrated above

The oyster mushrooms in this recipe make a pleasant change from the more usual button or flat mushrooms. They have a very attractive appearance, and are therefore kept whole in this dish.

PREPARATION TIME: 10 mins

COOKING TIME: 15 mins (plus 10 mins for the pasta)

SERVES 4

METHOD

1 For the sauce, melt the margarine in a medium-sized saucepan. Stir in the flour. Cook over a medium heat for 3 minutes until the roux is frothy and light in colour. Gradually add the milk, stirring well between each addition. Bring to the boil.

2 Add the mushrooms and dill weed and stir well until coated with sauce. Reduce the heat, cover, and simmer for 10 minutes, stirring occasionally, until the mushrooms are cooked.

3 Meanwhile, cook the macaroni by simmering in the water with the lemon juice, for 10 minutes. Drain well, season the sauce to taste and pour it over the macaroni. Mix well and serve.

PARMESAN FUSILLI IN ■ MUSHROOMS ■

INGREDIENTS

■ 1 tbsp (15ml) olive oil
■ 1 onion, finely chopped
■ 1 clove garlic, crushed
■ 4 large open mushrooms
■ 2 tsp (10ml) paprika
■ 2 tsp (10ml) chopped fresh thyme
■ ½ oz (15g) unbleached plain white flour
■ ¼ pint (150ml) stock
■ 14oz (400g) can of chopped tomatoes
■ 1 tbsp (15ml) tomato purée
■ salt and pepper
■ 12oz (375g) wholemeal fusilli
■ 5 pints (3 litres) water
■ 1 tsp (5ml) lemon juice
■ ½ pint (300ml) soured cream
■ 1oz (25g) grated Parmesan cheese
■ 2oz (50g) fresh wholemeal breadcrumbs

Illustrated right

Soured cream, mushrooms and pasta add up to a very tasty combination in this attractive recipe.
PREPARATION TIME: 30 mins
COOKING TIME: 25 mins (plus 10 mins for the pasta)
SERVES 4

METHOD

1 Heat the oil and fry the onion and garlic for 5 minutes. Finely chop the mushroom stalks and add to the onion mixture, with the paprika and thyme. Cook for 5 minutes, stirring occasionally.
2 Add the flour and cook for 1 minute. Pour in the stock and bring to the boil. Add the tomatoes and tomato purée, stirring constantly until the tomatoes are cooked. Season to taste.
3 Cook the fusilli by simmering in the water with the lemon juice, for 10 minutes. Mix two-thirds of the fusilli with the sauce. Put into a greased ovenproof dish.
4 Arrange the mushrooms on the sauce and fill with the remaining fusilli and soured cream. Mix together the Parmesan cheese and breadcrumbs and sprinkle over the fusilli. Bake in a preheated oven at Gas Mark 6, 400°F, 200°C for 25 minutes.

PASTA SHELLS WITH ■ SMOKED TOFU ■

INGREDIENTS

■ 12oz (375g) wholemeal pasta shells
■ 5 pints (3 litres) water
■ 2–3 tbsp (30–45ml) lemon juice
■ 2 tsp (10ml) sunflower oil
■ 8 spring onions, sliced
■ 2 cloves garlic, crushed
■ 1 tbsp (15ml) chopped fresh root ginger
■ 2 tbsp (30ml) tomato purée
■ 2 tbsp (30ml) cider vinegar
■ 1–2 tsp (5–10ml) honey
■ 8oz (250g) smoked tofu (bean curd), cut into cubes
■ salt and pepper

GARNISH
■ 2 tbsp (30ml) chopped fresh parsley

Illustrated right

Despite tofu's high-protein, low-fat qualities, many people find the taste too bland. Smoked tofu, used here, has a more distinctive flavour and may be a more attractive alternative.
PREPARATION TIME: 10 mins
COOKING TIME: 10 mins
SERVES 4

METHOD

1 Cook the pasta shells by simmering in the water with 1 tsp (5ml) lemon juice, for 10 minutes.
2 Meanwhile, for the sauce, heat the oil and fry the onions, garlic and ginger for 2 minutes. Add the remaining lemon juice, tomato purée, vinegar, honey and tofu and mix well. Cook gently for a further 5 minutes. Season to taste.
3 When the pasta is cooked, drain well. Mix with the sauce and serve garnished with chopped fresh parsley.

FROM LEFT: Parmesan fusilli in mushrooms; Pasta shells in peanut butter sauce

PASTA SHELLS IN PEANUT
■ BUTTER SAUCE ■

INGREDIENTS

■ 12oz (375g) wholemeal pasta shells
■ 6 pints (3.6 litres) water
■ 2 tbsp (30ml) lemon juice
■ 3 tbsp (45ml) smooth peanut butter
■ 1 tbsp (15ml) groundnut oil
■ 1oz (25g) plain wholemeal flour
■ 1 tbsp (15ml) lemon juice
■ 2 tbsp (30ml) tomato purée
■ 2 tsp (10ml) chopped fresh thyme
■ ¼ pint (150ml) pineapple juice
■ 1 tbsp (15ml) soya sauce
■ few drops Tabasco sauce
■ salt and pepper

GARNISH
■ 2 tbsp (30ml) chopped fresh parsley

Illustrated left

Natural peanut butter is a highly nutritious food, and forms the basis of the sauce below. It is now readily available, and should be used whenever possible, as other varieties are too sweet.
PREPARATION TIME: 10 mins
COOKING TIME: 5 mins (plus 10 mins for the pasta)
SERVES 4

METHOD

1 Cook the pasta shells by simmering in 5 pints (3 litres) of water and 1 tsp (5ml) lemon juice, for 10 minutes.
2 Meanwhile, make the sauce by combining the peanut butter with the oil in a saucepan. Stir in the flour and cook over a low heat for 3 minutes. Gradually add the remaining water and bring to the boil, stirring constantly (the mixture may appear to curdle at first). Add the remaining lemon juice, tomato purée, thyme, pineapple juice, soya sauce and Tabasco. Season to taste. Return to the boil and simmer for 5 minutes, stirring to allow the flavours to mingle. Mix the pasta with the sauce and garnish with parsley.

FROM LEFT: Pasta shells with smoked tofu; Pasta shells and flageolet beans

PASTA SHELLS AND
■ FLAGEOLET BEANS ■

INGREDIENTS

■ 6oz (175g) flageolet beans, soaked, or a 15oz (430g) can, drained
■ 1½oz (40g) butter or margarine
■ 1 onion, finely chopped
■ 1 clove garlic, crushed
■ 1½oz (40g) plain wholemeal flour
■ 1½ pints (900ml) milk
■ 1 tbsp (15ml) chopped fresh coriander
■ salt and pepper
■ 12oz (375g) wholemeal pasta shells
■ 5 pints (3 litres) water
■ 1 tsp (5ml) lemon juice

Illustrated above

Flageolet beans break up easily when overcooked, so cook the sauce carefully. If using canned beans, omit step 1 of the method.
PREPARATION TIME: 20 mins (plus 10–12 hours soaking time)
COOKING TIME: 50 mins for the beans (plus 10 mins for the pasta)
SERVES 4

METHOD

1 Boil the beans fast for 10 minutes, simmer for 40 minutes, then drain.
2 Heat the butter and fry the onion and garlic for 5 minutes. Add the beans and cook for 5 minutes. Add the flour and cook for 3 minutes, stirring constantly. Gradually add the milk and bring to the boil. Stir in the coriander and simmer for 5 minutes. Season to taste.
3 Cook the pasta in the water and lemon juice, for 10 minutes. Drain. Mix with the bean sauce and serve.

75

Fusilli with orange and avocado sauce

FUSILLI WITH ORANGE AND AVOCADO SAUCE

INGREDIENTS

- 12oz (375g) wholemeal fusilli
- 5 pints (3 litres) water
- 1 tsp (5ml) lemon juice
- 2 oranges
- 2 ripe avocados
- ½ tsp ground cinnamon
- 1 tsp (5ml) wholegrain mustard
- salt and pepper

GARNISH

- strips of orange rind

Illustrated above

The creamy, buttery texture of avocados makes them ideal for thickening sauces even though they are rather high in fat.

PREPARATION TIME: 10 mins
COOKING TIME: 10 mins
SERVES 4

METHOD

1 Cook the fusilli by simmering in the water with the lemon juice, for 10 minutes.
2 Meanwhile, make the sauce by puréeing the grated rind and juice of 1 orange, the flesh of 1 avocado, the cinnamon and mustard. Slice the flesh of the other avocado into bite-sized pieces and toss in the juice of the remaining orange.
3 Drain the fusilli. Combine with the sauce and avocado and orange juice. Season to taste. Serve immediately.

BASIC PASTA DOUGH

INGREDIENTS

- 1lb (500g) strong plain wholemeal flour
- 9fl oz (275ml) water

Pasta is traditionally made from refined durum wheat flour, but wholemeal flour can be used very successfully. Choose a strong flour that is described as "100 per cent wholemeal" – preferably stoneground and made from organically grown wheat. Eggs and salt make a rich pasta dough, but for a pasta that is lower in fat, use water instead of eggs, and the salt can be left out entirely. Make the dough in large quantities and then freeze the surplus for up to 3 months.

PREPARATION TIME: 50 mins
MAKES: 1½lb (750g) pasta dough
SERVES 8

METHOD

1 Put the flour into a mixing bowl and make a well in the centre. Pour in the water, mixing with a knife until the dough binds.
2 Mix with your hands and knead until all the flour has been incorporated (the dough will seem too dry at first).
3 Turn out on to a work surface and knead for about 10 minutes until the dough is smooth and elastic.
4 Cover the dough with clingfilm, or put into a polythene bag, and leave to rest for 30 minutes before rolling out.
5 If rolling out by hand, roll out a quarter of the dough at a time on a lightly floured surface. Roll as thinly as possible. Leave to rest and dry out slightly before using.

COURGETTE AND TOMATO LASAGNE

INGREDIENTS

■ 6oz (175g) wholemeal lasagne or ¼ quantity of pasta dough (see p.76)
■ 5 pints (3 litres) water
■ 1 tsp (5ml) lemon juice
■ 1 tbsp (15ml) olive oil
■ 1 onion, finely chopped
■ 1 clove garlic, crushed
■ 1lb (500g) courgettes, sliced
■ 14oz (400g) can of chopped tomatoes
■ ½ pint (300ml) stock (see p.49)
■ 1–2 tbsp (15–30ml) chopped fresh basil
■ 1 tbsp (15ml) soya sauce
■ 1½oz (40g) margarine or butter
■ 1oz (25g) plain wholemeal flour
■ ¾ pint (450ml) skimmed milk
■ ¼ tsp paprika
■ salt and pepper
■ 2oz (50g) Cheddar cheese, grated

Illustrated right

Using skimmed milk for the white sauce, and using cheese only on the top reduces the fat content of this dish considerably.

PREPARATION TIME: 40 mins (plus 40 mins for making the pasta)
COOKING TIME: 30 mins (plus 20 mins for cooking the pasta)
SERVES 4

METHOD

1 If using homemade lasagne, cook by simmering the water and lemon juice, for 4 minutes (16 minutes for dried pasta). Keep moist in a bowl of cold water.
2 For the courgette sauce, heat the oil and fry the onion and the garlic for 5 minutes. Add the courgettes and cook for a further 5 minutes. Add the tomatoes and stock. Simmer for 20 minutes until cooked. Stir in the basil and soya sauce.
3 For the white sauce, melt the margarine, stir in the flour and cook over a medium heat for 2–3 minutes, stirring constantly. Gradually add the skimmed milk and boil, stirring all the time, then simmer for 5 minutes. Add the paprika and season.
4 Grease a 3 pint (1.8 litre) ovenproof dish. Spread about 4 tbsp (60ml) white sauce over the bottom. Then layer alternately with lasagne and courgette and tomato sauce, ending with lasagne. Cover with the remaining white sauce and sprinkle with cheese. Bake in a preheated oven at Gas Mark 5, 375°F, 190°C for 30 minutes.

CLOCKWISE FROM TOP RIGHT: Courgette and tomato lasagne; Lasagne with garden pea sauce (see p.78); Lasagne verde with fennel (see p.78)

LASAGNE WITH
■ GARDEN PEA SAUCE ■

INGREDIENTS

■ 6oz (175g)
wholemeal lasagne
or ¼ quantity of
pasta dough (see
p.76)
■ 1 tbsp (15ml)
sunflower oil
■ 1lb (500g) onions,
chopped
■ 1 small potato,
diced
■ 1¼ pints (750ml)
milk
■ 1lb (500g) frozen
peas or shelled fresh
peas
■ 1 tbsp (15ml)
chopped fresh mint
■ salt and pepper
■ 1½oz (40g) butter
■ 1oz (25g) plain
wholemeal flour
■ ½ tsp mustard
powder
■ 3oz (75g) Cheddar
cheese, grated
■ grated Parmesan
cheese

Illustrated on page 77

Frozen peas can be used when fresh peas
are out of season.
PREPARATION TIME: 35 mins (plus 40 mins
for the pasta)
COOKING TIME: 40 mins (plus 16 mins for
the pasta)
SERVES 4

METHOD

1 Cook the lasagne (see recipe p.79). For
the pea sauce, heat the oil and fry the
onions for 5 minutes. Add the potato, ½
pint (300ml) milk and peas and bring to the
boil. Cover and simmer for 20 minutes.
Add the mint, season to taste and purée.
2 For the cheese sauce, melt the butter in a
small pan. Add the flour. Cook over a
medium heat, stirring constantly, for 3
minutes. Add the mustard powder.
Gradually add the remaining milk and
boil, stirring constantly. Reduce the heat
and simmer until the sauce thickens.
Remove from the heat, stir in the grated
Cheddar cheese and season to taste.
3 Grease a 3 pint (1.8 litre) ovenproof
dish. Spread 4 tbsp (60ml) cheese sauce
over the bottom. Layer alternately with
lasagne and pea sauce, ending with
lasagne. Cover with the remaining cheese
sauce and sprinkle with Parmesan. Bake in
a preheated oven at Gas Mark 6, 400°F,
200°C for 40 minutes.

LASAGNE VERDE WITH
■ FENNEL ■

INGREDIENTS

■ 6oz (175g) lasagne
verde or ¼ quantity
of pasta dough (see
p.76)
■ 1 tbsp (15ml)
sunflower oil
■ 1¼lb (625g)
fennel, roughly
chopped
■ 8oz (250g) celery
sticks, sliced
■ 2 tsp (10ml)
aniseeds
■ 1¼ pints (750ml)
milk
■ salt and pepper
■ 1½ oz (40g) butter
■ 1oz (25g) plain
wholemeal flour
■ ½ tsp mustard
powder
■ 3oz (75g) Cheddar
cheese, grated
■ grated Parmesan
cheese

Illustrated on page 77

Fennel and aniseed give a delicious subtle
flavour to this dish.
PREPARATION TIME: 35 mins (plus 40 mins
for the pasta)
COOKING TIME: 40 mins (plus 16 mins for
the pasta)
SERVES 4

METHOD

1 Cook the lasagne (see recipe p.79). For
the fennel sauce, heat the oil and fry the
fennel, celery and aniseeds for 5 minutes.
Add ½ pint (300ml) milk. Boil, cover and
simmer for 10 minutes. Purée until
smooth. Season to taste.
2 For the cheese sauce, melt the butter in a
small pan. Add the flour. Cook over a
medium heat, stirring constantly, for 3
minutes. Add the mustard powder.
Gradually add the remaining milk and
boil, stirring constantly. Reduce the heat
and simmer until the sauce thickens.
Remove from the heat, stir in the grated
Cheddar cheese and season to taste.
3 Grease a 3 pint (1.8 litre) ovenproof
dish. Spread 4 tbsp (60ml) cheese sauce
over the bottom. Layer alternately with
lasagne and fennel sauce, ending with
lasagne. Cover with the remaining cheese
sauce and sprinkle with Parmesan. Bake in
a preheated oven at Gas Mark 6, 400°F,
200°C for 40 minutes.

MAKING LASAGNE

*L*asagne is the name for large flat strips of pasta, which you can buy plain, wholemeal or green (flavoured with spinach and called lasagne verde). There is also a type of lasagne which does not require pre-cooking, now available from supermarkets.

1 *Make the basic pasta dough (see p.76). Leave to rest for 30 minutes. Roll out a quarter of the dough.*

2 *When the dough is rolled thinly into a large square, trim the edges.*

3 *Cut into rectangles measuring about 4 × 3 inches (10 × 7cm). Cook as directed in the recipe you are using.*

CARROT AND SPLIT PEA CANNELLONI

INGREDIENTS

- 6oz (175g) cannelloni (about 16 tubes) or ¼ quantity of pasta dough (see p.76)
- 1 tbsp (15ml) sunflower oil
- 1 onion, chopped
- 12oz (375g) carrots, sliced
- 6oz (175g) yellow split peas
- 1 pint (600ml) water
- 2 tsp (10ml) chopped fresh sage
- ¾ pint (450ml) skimmed milk
- 1 small potato, diced
- 1 bunch watercress
- 2oz (50g) fresh wholemeal breadcrumbs
- 1oz (25g) grated Parmesan cheese

Illustrated on page 80

The split peas and skimmed milk in this dish combine well to make a nutritious but low-fat meal.

PREPARATION TIME: 1 hour 25 mins (plus 40 mins for making the pasta)
COOKING TIME: 40 mins
SERVES 4

METHOD

1 If using homemade cannelloni, cut the rolled-out pasta dough into rectangles measuring 4×3 inches (10×7cm).
2 For the stuffing, heat the oil in a medium-sized saucepan and fry the onion for 5 minutes until soft but not browned.
3 Add the carrots and split peas and cook gently for a further 5 minutes, stirring occasionally to allow the flavours to mingle.
4 Add the water and sage. Bring to the boil. Reduce the heat and simmer for 30 minutes until the split peas are cooked.
5 Meanwhile, for the sauce, put the skimmed milk and potato into a pan and bring to the boil. Add the watercress and return to the boil. Reduce the heat, cover and simmer for 20 minutes until the potato is tender. Allow the sauce to cool slightly, then put in a blender or food processor and liquidise until smooth.
6 When the stuffing mixture is cooked, allow it to cool slightly, then place in a blender or food processor and liquidise until smooth. If the filling is too wet, return to the pan and dry it out over a low heat, stirring occasionally.
7 For homemade cannelloni, put 2 tbsp (30ml) of the filling on each pasta rectangle. Moisten the edges and roll up into a tube shape. Alternatively, fill the ready-formed tubes.
8 Put the filled cannelloni into a greased ovenproof dish and cover with the watercress sauce.
9 For the topping, mix the breadcrumbs with the Parmesan cheese. Sprinkle it over the cannelloni. Bake in a preheated oven at Gas Mark 5, 375°F, 190°C for 40 minutes until the top is lightly browned.

CANNELLONI WITH ■ NUT STUFFING ■

INGREDIENTS

■ 6oz (175g) cannelloni (about 16 tubes) or ¼ quantity of pasta dough (see p.76)
■ 2oz (50g) margarine or butter
■ 1½oz (40g) plain wholemeal flour
■ 1½ pints (900ml) skimmed milk
■ 6oz (175g) button mushrooms, chopped
■ 4oz (125g) ground hazelnuts
■ 2oz (50g) ground Brazil nuts
■ 4oz (125g) medium oatmeal
■ 2 tsp (10ml) chopped fresh thyme
■ salt and pepper

Illustrated right

If you are not making homemade cannelloni, use the no-pre-cook cannelloni tubes as they are easier to work with. This dish uses oatmeal – a particularly valuable type of fibre.

PREPARATION TIME: 35 mins (plus 40 mins for the pasta)
COOKING TIME: 35 mins
SERVES 4

METHOD

1 If using homemade cannelloni, roll out the pasta dough and cut into rectangles measuring 4×3 inches (10×7cm).
2 For the sauce, melt the margarine. Stir in the flour and cook for 3 minutes over a medium heat. Gradually add the milk. Boil, stirring. Add the mushrooms. Return to the boil, cover, and simmer for 10 minutes.
3 For the stuffing, mix together the ground nuts, oatmeal and thyme. Add half the mushroom sauce, season and mix well.
4 For homemade cannelloni, put 2 tbsp (30ml) of the nut stuffing on each pasta rectangle. Moisten the edges and roll up into a tube shape. Alternatively, stuff the ready-formed tubes. Put into a greased ovenproof dish. Add the remaining sauce and bake in a preheated oven at Gas Mark 5, 375°F, 190°C for 35 minutes.

CLOCKWISE FROM TOP LEFT: Pea and ginger cannelloni; Carrot and split pea cannelloni (see p.79); Buckwheat and cabbage cannelloni; Cannelloni with nut stuffing

PEA AND GINGER CANNELLONI

INGREDIENTS

■ 6oz (175g) cannelloni (about 16 tubes) or ¼ quantity of pasta dough (see p.76)
■ 12oz (375g) frozen peas
■ 1 tbsp (15ml) olive oil
■ 1 large onion, finely chopped
■ 1 clove garlic, crushed
■ 1 tsp (5ml) cumin seeds
■ 1 tbsp (15ml) grated fresh root ginger
■ 1 tbsp (15ml) lemon juice
■ 14oz (400g) can of chopped tomatoes
■ 1 tbsp (15ml) soya sauce
■ salt and pepper

Illustrated left

This mildly spiced filling has an Indian flavour to it.

PREPARATION TIME: 20 mins (plus 40 mins for the pasta)

COOKING TIME: 40 mins

SERVES 4

METHOD

1 If using homemade cannelloni, cut the rolled-out pasta dough into rectangles measuring 4×3 inches (10×7cm). Cook the peas according to the directions on the packet.
2 Heat the oil and fry the onion and garlic for 5 minutes. Add the cumin, ginger and peas to half the onion mixture and cook gently for 5 minutes. Add the lemon juice and enough water to make a moist mixture. Remove from the heat and season to taste.
3 For homemade cannelloni, put 2 tbsp (30ml) of the stuffing on each pasta rectangle. Moisten the edges and roll up into a tube shape. Alternatively, stuff the ready-formed tubes. Put into a greased ovenproof dish.
4 For the sauce, purée the tomatoes, soya sauce and remaining onion mixture. Pour over the cannelloni and bake in a preheated oven at Gas Mark 5, 375°F, 190°C for 40 minutes.

BUCKWHEAT AND CABBAGE CANNELLONI

INGREDIENTS

■ 6oz (175g) cannelloni (about 16 tubes) or ¼ quantity of pasta dough (see p.76)
■ 2 tsp (10ml) sunflower oil
■ 1 onion, finely chopped
■ 1 clove garlic, crushed
■ 5oz (150g) buckwheat
■ 5oz (150g) red cabbage, finely chopped
■ 1½ pints (900ml) water
■ 2 tsp (10ml) chopped fresh dill
■ 2oz (50g) dried apricots
■ salt and pepper

Illustrated left

You could use either roasted or unroasted buckwheat in this recipe.

PREPARATION TIME: 1 hour (plus 40 mins for the pasta)

COOKING TIME: 40 mins

SERVES 4

METHOD

1 If using homemade cannelloni, cut the rolled-out pasta dough into rectangles measuring 4×3 inches (10×7cm).
2 For the stuffing, heat the oil and fry the onion and garlic for 5 minutes. Add the buckwheat and cabbage and cook for 5 minutes. Add ¾ pint (450ml) water and the dill. Cover and simmer for 20 minutes.
3 For the sauce, put the apricots in a pan with the remaining water. Boil, cover and simmer, for 20 minutes, then purée. Season to taste.
4 For homemade cannelloni, put 2 tbsp (30ml) of the stuffing on each pasta rectangle. Moisten the edges and roll up into a tube shape. Alternatively, stuff the ready-formed tubes.
5 Transfer the stuffed cannelloni to a greased ovenproof dish and pour the sauce on top. Bake in a preheated oven at Gas Mark 5, 375°F, 190°C for 40 minutes.

CASSEROLES ❚ AND BAKES ❚

CLOCKWISE FROM TOP: Smooth and crunchy courgettes (see p.85); Sweet and sour hazelnuts (see p.84); Cashew nut moussaka (see p.84)

SWEET AND SOUR ■ HAZELNUTS ■

INGREDIENTS

RISSOLES
■ 4oz (125g)
hazelnuts, ground
■ 4oz (125g)
wholemeal
breadcrumbs
■ 1 onion, finely
chopped
■ 1 clove garlic,
crushed
■ 2 tsp (10ml) mixed
fresh herbs
■ 1 tsp (5ml) yeast
extract
■ ¼ pint (150ml)
boiling water
■ 1 egg, beaten
■ 5 tbsp (75ml) plain
wholemeal flour or
wholemeal
breadcrumbs

SAUCE
■ 2 tsp (10ml)
sunflower oil
■ 4oz (125g) celery,
trimmed and cut into
sticks
■ 4oz (125g) carrots,
cut into sticks
■ 1 red pepper,
deseeded and cut
into strips
■ ½ pint (300ml)
water
■ 2 tbsp (30ml)
arrowroot or
cornflour
■ 1 tbsp (15ml) soya
sauce
■ 1 tbsp (15ml) cider
vinegar
■ 2 tsp (10ml) clear
honey
■ 2 tbsp (30ml)
tomato purée
■ salt and pepper

GARNISH
■ celery leaves

Illustrated on page 83

Small rissoles made from hazelnuts and
herbs are served here in a delicious sweet
and sour sauce. The rissoles could be fried,
but for a healthier dish, bake them in the
oven. Serve with rice or jacket potatoes and
a crisp, green salad.

PREPARATION TIME: 40 mins
COOKING TIME: 20 mins
SERVES 4

METHOD

1 Mix together the hazelnuts,
breadcrumbs, onion, garlic and mixed
herbs in a large bowl.
2 Dissolve the yeast extract in the boiling
water and add to the hazelnut mixture to
give a moist consistency.
3 Divide the mixture into 12 small rissoles.
Dip each one into the beaten egg and then
into the flour or breadcrumbs. Put the
rissoles on a lightly oiled baking tray.
4 Bake in a preheated oven at Gas Mark 5,
375°F, 190°C for 20 minutes, turning once
during the cooking time.
5 For the sauce, heat the oil in a medium
pan and gently cook the celery, carrots and
pepper for 10 minutes.
6 In a bowl, mix a little of the water with
the arrowroot or cornflour to form a thick
paste and stir in the rest of the water. Add
the soya sauce, cider vinegar, honey and
tomato purée. Mix well.
7 Pour the tomato mixture over the
vegetables. Bring to the boil, stirring all the
time. Continue cooking until the sauce
thickens and becomes clear. Simmer gently
for a further 5–10 minutes until the
vegetables are just tender. Season to taste.
8 Add the hazelnut rissoles to the sauce,
warm through gently and serve garnished
with celery leaves.

■ CASHEW NUT MOUSSAKA ■

INGREDIENTS

■ 1 large aubergine,
thinly sliced
■ 1 tbsp (15ml) olive
oil
■ 1 onion, chopped
■ 1 clove garlic,
crushed
■ 4oz (125g)
mushrooms, sliced
■ 1 green pepper,
deseeded and sliced
■ 2oz (50g) unsalted
cashew nuts, roughly
chopped if large
■ 1oz (25g)
wholemeal
breadcrumbs
■ 1 tbsp (15ml)
tomato purée
■ 2 tsp (10ml)
chopped fresh basil
■ 1 tbsp (15ml) soya
sauce
■ ¼ pint (150ml)
water
■ salt and pepper
■ 1oz (25g) plain
wholemeal flour
■ ½ pint (300ml)
skimmed milk
■ 1 egg
■ 2oz (50g) Cheddar
cheese, grated
■ 2 tsp (10ml) grated
Parmesan cheese

GARNISH
■ tomato segments

Illustrated on page 83

Traditionally, moussakas are very high in
fat, because aubergines absorb a lot of oil in
cooking. However, here they are baked in
very little oil, and the white sauce is made
without any fat.

PREPARATION TIME: 50 mins
COOKING TIME: 40 mins
SERVES 4

METHOD

1 Put the aubergine slices on to a large
baking tray which has been lightly brushed
with ½ teaspoon of the oil. Brush the tops
of the aubergine slices with another ½
teaspoon of the oil. Bake in a preheated
oven at Gas Mark 5, 375°F, 190°C for 10
minutes. Remove from the oven and set
aside.
2 Heat the remaining oil in a large frying
pan and gently fry the onion and garlic for
4–5 minutes. Add the mushrooms and
pepper, cover and cook gently for a
further 10 minutes.
3 Stir in the cashew nuts, breadcrumbs,
tomato purée, basil, soya sauce and
sufficient water to make a moist mixture.
Check the seasoning.
4 Put approximately half the onion and
nut mixture into the base of a large
casserole or ovenproof dish. Top with half
of the aubergine slices. Then put in the
remaining onion mixture and cover with
the rest of the aubergine slices.
5 Mix the flour, milk and egg in a blender
or food processor until smooth.
Alternatively, put the flour into a large
bowl, beat the egg with the milk, then
gradually beat into the flour.
6 Put the milk mixture into a small pan
and slowly bring to the boil, stirring
continuously. Simmer for 3–4 minutes
until thickened, stirring continuously.
Remove from the heat and stir in the
Cheddar cheese. Check the seasoning.
7 Pour the cheese sauce over the
aubergine mixture. Sprinkle with
Parmesan cheese. Cover the dish.
8 Bake in the oven for 35–40 minutes,
uncovered for the last 10 minutes. Serve
hot garnished with tomato segments.

SMOOTH AND CRUNCHY ▌ COURGETTES ▌

INGREDIENTS

- 1 tbsp (15ml) sunflower oil
- 1lb (500g) courgettes, sliced
- 2 cloves garlic, crushed
- 4oz (125g) mushrooms, sliced
- 1 tsp (5ml) chopped fresh basil
- 14oz (400g) can of chopped tomatoes
- 2oz (50g) bulgar wheat
- 2oz (50g) unsalted cashew nuts
- ¼ pint (150ml) smetana, soured cream or natural yogurt
- salt and pepper

Illustrated on page 83

Smetana, a cultured skimmed-milk product, is low in fat, yet creamy and full of flavour. Here it is used to make a delicious combination with courgettes, cashew nuts and bulgar wheat. This kind of wheat is made from whole grains that have been soaked and then baked until they crack.

PREPARATION TIME: 15 mins
COOKING TIME: 10 mins
SERVES 4

METHOD

1 Heat the oil in a large frying pan and gently fry the courgettes and garlic for 5 minutes. Add the mushrooms, cover and cook for 5 minutes.
2 Stir in the basil, tomatoes, bulgar wheat and cashew nuts. Cover and cook for a further 10 minutes.
3 Stir in the smetana, soured cream or yogurt, warm through gently and season to taste. Serve hot.

▌ HARVEST HOT POT ▌

INGREDIENTS

- 8oz (250g) pearl barley
- 2 tsp (10ml) sunflower oil
- 8oz (250g) shallots or small onions, peeled
- 2 small leeks, trimmed and sliced
- 1 large potato, diced
- 6oz (175g) carrots, sliced
- 6oz (175g) button mushrooms
- 2 tsp (10ml) chopped fresh rosemary
- 2 tsp (10ml) chopped fresh thyme
- 1 tsp (5ml) yeast extract
- salt and pepper

Illustrated right

Pearl barley makes a nutritious and interesting alternative to rice. Serve with a green vegetable and a sprig of thyme to garnish.

PREPARATION TIME: 45 mins
COOKING TIME: 30 mins
SERVES 4

METHOD

1 Cover the barley with plenty of water. Bring to the boil, cover and simmer for 30–40 minutes. Drain and reserve the stock.
2 Heat the oil in a large pan and gently fry the shallots, leeks, potato, carrots and mushrooms for 8–10 minutes. Add the rosemary, thyme and cooked barley.
3 Make the reserved stock up to ¾ pint (450ml) with water. Add to the barley and vegetables together with the yeast extract. Bring to the boil, cover and simmer for 30 minutes. Season to taste. Serve hot.

FROM LEFT: Harvest hot pot; Summer vegetables with golden millet; Winter vegetables with buckwheat (see p.86)

SUMMER VEGETABLES WITH ▌ GOLDEN MILLET ▌

INGREDIENTS

- 1 tbsp (15ml) sunflower oil
- 6oz (175g) millet
- 1 bunch spring onions, chopped
- 1 small green pepper, chopped
- 6oz (175g) courgettes, thickly sliced
- 4oz (125g) green beans, cut into 1 inch (2.5cm) pieces
- ½ pint (300ml) apple juice
- ½ pint (300ml) boiling water
- 2 tsp (10ml) chopped fresh thyme
- grated rind of 1 large lemon
- 2oz (50g) blanched almonds
- 4 medium tomatoes, cut into quarters
- salt and pepper

Illustrated above

Golden-coloured millet is a nutritious grain. Here it combines perfectly with summer vegetables, which could be varied according to availability. Garnish with tomato slices.

PREPARATION TIME: 30 mins
COOKING TIME: 20 mins
SERVES 4

METHOD

1 Heat the oil in a large pan and lightly toast the millet until it starts to become golden brown. Add the spring onions, pepper, courgettes and green beans and cook gently for 5–7 minutes.
2 Stir in the apple juice, boiling water, thyme and lemon rind. Bring to the boil, cover and simmer gently for 15–20 minutes until the millet is cooked.
3 Meanwhile toast the almonds under a preheated moderate grill, or in a preheated oven at Gas Mark 4, 350°F, 180°C for 4–5 minutes until golden brown. Roughly chop the toasted almonds.
4 Add the almonds and tomatoes to the millet. Season to taste. Serve hot or cold.

WINTER VEGETABLES WITH ❚ BUCKWHEAT ❚

INGREDIENTS

▮ 1 tbsp (15ml) sunflower oil
▮ 6oz (175g) unroasted or ready-roasted buckwheat
▮ 4oz (125g) red split lentils
▮ 1 large onion, finely chopped
▮ 1 clove garlic, crushed
▮ 6oz (175g) carrots, thinly sliced
▮ 8oz (250g) leeks, finely sliced
▮ 6oz (175g) parsnips, grated
▮ 2 tsp (10ml) chopped fresh rosemary
▮ 1 tsp (5ml) chopped fresh thyme
▮ 1 pint (600ml) boiling water
▮ 2 tbsp (30ml) soya sauce
▮ 3 tbsp (45ml) tahini
▮ salt and pepper

Illustrated on page 85

Buckwheat is a tasty and nutritious grain, available roasted or unroasted. If you are using ready-roasted buckwheat, simply put the oil in the pan with the buckwheat and lentils and move straight on to step 2. If you are using lentils that have not been ready-prepared, remember to rinse them well and pick over for stones. This dish can be served as a slice or as a loaf and then turned out. Serve hot with a mushroom or tomato sauce, or cold with salads.

PREPARATION TIME: 35 mins
COOKING TIME: 25–45 mins
SERVES 4

METHOD

1 Heat the oil over a moderate heat and gently cook the buckwheat and lentils for 5 minutes to lightly toast the buckwheat.
2 Add the onion and garlic and fry for 3 minutes. Add the carrots, leeks and parsnips, rosemary and thyme and cook for 5 minutes.
3 Add the boiling water, cover and simmer for 15 minutes. Stir in the soya sauce and tahini. Check the seasoning.
4 Put the mixture into a lightly oiled 12×8 inch (30×20cm) tin or a lined 1lb (500g) loaf tin. Bake in a preheated oven at Gas Mark 4, 350°F, 180°C for 25 minutes if using a rectangular tin, or 45 minutes if using the loaf tin. Serve hot or cold.

FROM LEFT: Brazil nut rissoles; Tofu patties

❚ TOFU PATTIES ❚

INGREDIENTS

▮ 1 aubergine, 8oz (250g) in weight
▮ 8oz (250g) firm tofu (bean curd)
▮ 1oz (25g) creamed coconut, grated
▮ 3oz (75g) breadcrumbs
▮ 2 tbsp (30ml) tomato purée
▮ 4 tsp (20ml) soya sauce
▮ 1–2 cloves garlic, crushed
▮ 2–3 tbsp (30–45ml) chopped coriander
▮ 1 tsp (5ml) ground cumin
▮ ½–1 tsp (2.5–5ml) turmeric
▮ salt and pepper
▮ 1oz (25g) wheatgerm
▮ 1oz (25g) bran
▮ oil for frying

Illustrated above

Use firm tofu (bean curd) for these tasty patties because it mashes easily and mixes well with the other ingredients.

PREPARATION TIME: 30 mins
COOKING TIME: 15 mins
MAKES: 8 patties

METHOD

1 Prick the aubergine skin and cut off the stalk and leaves. Bake in a preheated oven at Gas Mark 4, 350°F, 180°C for 20–25 minutes or until soft. Scoop out the flesh and purée until smooth.
2 Blend the tofu and coconut until smooth. Stir in the breadcrumbs, tomato purée, soya sauce, garlic, spices and the aubergine. Season well. Leave until firm.
3 Make into eight patties and if frying, roll them in a mixture of wheatgerm and bran. Gently fry for 3–4 minutes on each side, or bake in a hot oven at Gas Mark 6, 400°F, 200°C for 15 minutes, turning during the cooking. Serve hot.

▌ BRAZIL NUT RISSOLES ▌

INGREDIENTS

- 2oz (50g) short-grain brown rice
- 1 tbsp (15ml) olive oil
- 6oz (175g) leeks, trimmed and diced
- 1 tsp (5ml) celery seeds
- 6oz (175g) flat mushrooms, diced
- 4oz (125g) Brazil nuts, ground
- 1oz (25g) walnut pieces, ground
- 1 egg, beaten
- 1 tsp (5ml) yeast extract
- 2 tbsp (30ml) chopped fresh parsley
- 1 tsp (5ml) paprika
- salt and pepper
- oil for shallow frying

Illustrated left

The mixture of rice and nuts in these rissoles makes them a good source of protein. The grains add texture and fibre while the Brazil nuts provide a creamy richness that works well with the stronger walnut flavour.

PREPARATION TIME: 45 mins
COOKING TIME: 7–20 mins
MAKES: 8–10 rissoles

METHOD

1 Cook the rice in twice its volume of boiling water for 25–35 minutes or until very tender.
2 Heat the oil and gently fry the leeks for 5–7 minutes. Add the celery seeds and mushrooms and cook for another 10 minutes. Drain off any excess liquid.
3 Remove from the heat and mix in the rice and remaining ingredients. Season well. The consistency should be moist enough to hold together. Add a little stock if necessary.
4 Shape into eight or ten rissoles and shallow fry for 5–7 minutes. Alternatively, bake in a preheated oven at Gas Mark 4, 350°F, 180°C for 20 minutes, turn after 10 minutes.

Walnut and buckwheat goulash

WALNUT AND BUCKWHEAT ▌ GOULASH ▌

INGREDIENTS

STOCK
- 2 tsp (10ml) sunflower oil
- 1 onion, peeled and finely chopped
- 8oz (250g) mushrooms, wiped and chopped
- ¼ pint (150ml) water
- ¼ pint (150ml) red wine

GOULASH
- 1 tbsp (15ml) sunflower oil
- 1 onion, peeled and finely chopped
- 8oz (250g) celeriac, peeled and diced
- 8oz (250g) carrots, scrubbed and diced
- 8oz (250g) parsnips, scrubbed and diced
- 4oz (125g) walnut pieces
- 2 tsp (10ml) caraway seeds
- 4oz (125g) buckwheat
- 2 tsp (10ml) soya sauce
- black pepper

GARNISH
- soured cream or smetana
- pinch of paprika

Illustrated left

This rich, dark stew combines the flavours of walnut and buckwheat with a thick wine and mushroom stock. Nuts and grains served together are a useful source of protein and the textures complement each other. The Latin name for walnut, "juglans regia", means "fit for a king" and it has been known as the Royal Nut in the past. Its rich but unobtrusive flavour enhances the chewy texture of the buckwheat.

PREPARATION TIME: 1 hour
COOKING TIME: 30 mins
SERVES 4

METHOD

1 For the stock, heat the oil in a pan and lightly fry the onion for 2–3 minutes. Add the mushrooms and cook for a further 2–3 minutes, then pour in the water and wine.
2 Simmer for 15 minutes until the vegetables are completely soft. Purée in a blender or food processor until smooth.
3 For the goulash, heat the oil in another pan and gently fry the onion for 3–4 minutes or until soft.
4 Add the celeriac, carrots, parsnips, nuts, caraway seeds and buckwheat, and stew for 10 minutes.
5 Stir in the mushroom stock and simmer for 30 minutes, adding more liquid if necessary. Season with soya sauce and pepper.
6 Serve with soured cream or smetana and a dusting of paprika.

Kidney bean and parsnip bake

KIDNEY BEAN AND
■ PARSNIP BAKE ■

INGREDIENTS

■ 8oz (250g) dried
red kidney beans,
soaked, or a 15oz
(430g) can, drained
■ 12oz (375g)
parsnips, scrubbed
■ 1 tbsp (15ml)
sunflower oil
■ 8oz (250g) leeks,
trimmed and
chopped
■ 1 clove garlic,
crushed
■ 2oz (50g) porridge
oats
■ 2 tbsp (30ml) soya
sauce
■ 2 tbsp (30ml)
tomato purée
■ 2 tbsp (30ml)
chopped fresh
parsley
■ 1 tsp (5ml) caraway
seeds
■ 1 tsp (5ml) allspice
■ salt and pepper

Illustrated above

Red kidney beans and parsnips go well
together, both having a slightly sweet
flavour. The porridge oats provide texture
and extra protein. If using canned beans,
omit step 1.

PREPARATION TIME: 35 mins (plus 10–12
hours soaking time)
COOKING TIME: 30–40 mins (plus 1 hour for
the beans)
SERVES 4–6

METHOD

1 Drain the beans and place in a saucepan
with plenty of fresh water. Boil fast for 10
minutes, then simmer for about 50
minutes. Drain the beans and set aside.
2 Steam the parsnips for 10–15 minutes.
Drain, reserving the liquid. Mash until
smooth.
3 Gently fry the leeks in the oil until soft,
add the garlic and beans and cook for 5
minutes. Mix with the parsnips and
remaining ingredients. Add a little stock to
moisten if necessary. Season to taste.
4 Spoon the mixture into a well-greased 9
inch (23cm) square baking tin or flan dish.
Bake in a preheated oven at Gas Mark 4,
350°F, 180°C for 30–40 minutes. Serve hot.

LENTILS AND COURGETTES
■ IN HERB SAUCE ■

INGREDIENTS

■ 6oz (175g) green
lentils
■ 3 pints (1.8 litres)
water
■ 1 tbsp (15ml)
sunflower oil
■ 1 onion, chopped
■ 2 sticks celery,
chopped
■ 8oz (250g)
courgettes, sliced
■ 4oz (125g) peas
■ 2 tbsp (30ml) plain
unbleached white
flour
■ ½ pint (300ml)
lentil stock
■ 2 tbsp (30ml)
chopped fresh
parsley
■ 3 tbsp (45ml)
chopped fresh mint
■ 2 tsp (10ml) fresh
oregano
■ 1 bay leaf
■ 2 tsp (10ml) soya
sauce
■ 1 tbsp (15ml) lemon
juice
■ salt and pepper

Illustrated right

This light vegetable casserole with its
creamy, herb-flavoured sauce is delicious
served with new potatoes and a crisp carrot
salad.

PREPARATION TIME: 50 mins
COOKING TIME: 15 mins
SERVES 4

METHOD

1 Wash the lentils, place in a pan with
plenty of water, bring to the boil and
simmer for 30 minutes. Drain, reserving ½
pint (300ml) stock.
2 Heat the oil in a pan and fry the onion
and celery for 5 minutes. Add the
courgettes, peas and cooked lentils.
Sprinkle on the flour and cook for 2–3
minutes.
3 Add the lentil stock, stirring well, then
the parsley, mint and oregano and a bay
leaf. Cook gently for 15 minutes. Stir in the
soya sauce and lemon juice. Check the
seasoning. Remove the bay leaf and
serve hot.

FROM TOP: *Lentils and courgettes in herb sauce; Aduki beans in a sweet and sour sauce*

ADUKI BEANS IN A SWEET AND SOUR SAUCE

INGREDIENTS

- 6oz (175g) dried aduki beans, soaked, or a 15oz (430g) can of red kidney beans, drained
- 1 tbsp (30ml) sunflower oil
- 1 onion, chopped
- 1 clove garlic, crushed
- 1 medium red pepper, deseeded and cut into thin strips
- 6oz (175g) sweetcorn, fresh, frozen or canned
- 2 tbsp (30ml) arrowroot or cornflour
- 1 tbsp (15ml) soya sauce
- 2 tbsp (30ml) cider vinegar
- 1 tbsp (15ml) clear honey
- 2 tbsp (30ml) tomato purée
- ½ pint (300ml) bean stock or water and a vegetable stock cube.

GARNISH

- cucumber strips
- few sprigs parsley

Illustrated left

Aduki beans cooked in a tangy sauce make a nutritious, high-fibre meal, especially when served with brown rice or wholemeal noodles. This recipe will be just as delicious if you substitute a 15oz (430g) can of red kidney beans for the aduki beans, in which case omit step 1.

PREPARATION TIME: 20 mins (plus 10–12 hours soaking time)
COOKING TIME: 10 mins (plus 50 mins for the beans)
SERVES 4

METHOD

1 Drain the beans. Place in a pan with plenty of fresh water. Bring to the boil and boil fast for 10 minutes. Reduce the heat, cover and simmer for 35 minutes. Drain reserving the liquid.

2 Heat the oil in a large pan and fry the onion and garlic for 5–8 minutes. Add the cooked beans, red pepper and sweetcorn and cook gently for 2–3 minutes.

3 Mix the arrowroot, soya sauce, cider vinegar, honey, tomato purée and 2–3 tbsp (30–45ml) of the bean stock into a smooth paste. Pour over the bean mixture, adding the rest of the bean stock.

4 Bring to the boil, reduce the heat and cook gently for about 5 minutes until the sauce becomes clear and glossy. Cook for a further 5 minutes. Serve hot, garnished with cucumber strips and sprigs of parsley.

CHILLI POLENTA WITH SPICY MUSHROOM SAUCE

INGREDIENTS

- ½ pint (300ml) skimmed milk
- ½ pint (300ml) water
- 1 bay leaf
- 12 black peppercorns
- 1 clove garlic, roughly chopped
- 4oz (125g) coarse cornmeal
- ½ tsp olive oil
- 2 tbsp (30ml) grated Parmesan cheese

SAUCE

- 1 tbsp (15ml) olive oil
- 1 large onion, chopped
- 1 clove garlic, crushed
- 1 fresh red chilli, deseeded and chopped
- 4oz (125g) mushrooms, sliced
- 2 tsp (10ml) paprika
- 2 tsp (10ml) chopped fresh thyme
- 14oz (400g) can of chopped tomatoes
- salt and pepper

Illustrated right

Polenta is a traditional Italian dish made with golden cornmeal. In this version the polenta is baked in the oven at a high temperature instead of fried. It is served with a spicy mushroom sauce and garnished with tomato. When using fresh chillis, do not include the stalk end and the seeds, unless you like the sauce really hot!

PREPARATION TIME: 1¼ hours
COOKING TIME: 15 mins
SERVES 4

METHOD

1 To make the polenta dough, put the milk, water, bay leaf, peppercorns and garlic in a small pan, and bring to the boil. Remove from the heat, cover and leave to stand for 20 minutes.

2 Strain into a jug. In a small bowl, mix a little of the strained milk mixture with the cornmeal to make a smooth paste. Gradually stir in the rest of the milk mixture. Return to the pan, bring to the boil and simmer for 10 minutes, stirring continuously.

3 Pour the polenta on to a greased baking tray and spread out to ½ inch (1cm) thickness. Set aside to cool.

4 For the sauce, heat the oil in a medium pan and gently fry the onion and garlic for 5 minutes. Add the chilli, mushrooms, paprika and thyme, and continue cooking for 5 minutes.

5 Drain the tomatoes, reserving the juice, and add to the onion mixture. Bring to the boil, cover and simmer for 25–30 minutes, adding a little extra tomato juice or water if necessary. Check the seasoning.

6 Cut the cold polenta into rounds or squares. Lightly oil a casserole or ovenproof dish and lay the polenta shapes in the dish so that they overlap. Sprinkle with the cheese. Bake in a preheated oven at Gas Mark 6, 400°F, 200°C for 15 minutes. Serve hot with the spicy mushroom sauce.

Chilli polenta with spicy mushroom sauce

BLACK EYE BEAN
■ PASTIES ■

INGREDIENTS

■ 6oz (175g) black
eye beans, soaked, or
15oz (430g) can,
drained

PASTRY
■ 8oz (250g) plain
wholemeal flour
■ ¼ tsp salt
■ 4oz (125g)
margarine
■ 5–6 tbsp (75–90ml)
water
■ 2 tsp (10ml)
sunflower oil
■ 2 tsp (10ml) lemon
juice

FILLING
■ 1 tbsp (15ml)
sunflower oil
■ 1 onion, peeled and
chopped
■ 6oz (175g)
mushrooms, wiped
and diced
■ 6oz (175g)
potatoes, scrubbed
and diced
■ 1 tsp (5ml) dried
marjoram
■ 1 tsp (5ml) dried
thyme
■ 2 tbsp (30ml)
chopped fresh
parsley
■ 2 tbsp (30ml) lemon
juice
■ soya sauce to taste
■ salt and pepper

GLAZE
■ a little beaten egg

Illustrated on page 92

These satisfying and versatile pasties are
good for lunch or supper. Black eye beans
are small, whitish beans with a distinctive
black or yellow "eye" and are a useful
ingredient because they absorb other
flavours. Black eye beans originated in
China, but are more often associated with
the American Deep South where they are
traditionally eaten with pork. The
immature pods and young shoots and
leaves are also edible. If using canned
beans, omit step 1 of the recipe.

PREPARATION TIME: 1 hour (plus 10–12
hours soaking time)
COOKING TIME: 15–20 mins (plus 45 mins
for the beans)
SERVES 8

METHOD

1 Drain the beans. Place in a pan with
plenty of fresh water and bring to the boil.
Boil fast for 10 minutes, then cover and
simmer for 35 minutes or until the beans
are soft. Drain.
2 Meanwhile, for the pastry, mix the flour
and salt together in a large bowl.
3 Rub in the margarine until the mixture
resembles fine breadcrumbs.
4 Mix the water, oil and lemon juice
together. Sprinkle over the flour mixture
and quickly draw to a soft dough.
5 Wrap the dough in clingfilm or a
polythene bag and chill for 20 minutes.
6 For the filling, heat the oil in a pan and
gently fry the onion for 3–4 minutes.
7 Add the mushrooms, potatoes, cooked
beans, herbs, lemon juice and soya sauce.
Cook very slowly for 10–15 minutes
adding a little water if necessary. Season to
taste and cool.
8 Roll out the pastry and cut into 8 rounds.
Place 1 tbsp (15ml) of filling on each round,
then fold over and seal the edges using
water. Prick a hole in each side and brush
with beaten egg.
9 Place the pasties on a greased baking
sheet. Bake in a preheated oven at Gas
Mark 6, 400°F, 200°C for 15–20 minutes.

■ MAKING PASTIES ■

*W*holemeal pastry parcels with a vegetable, bean
or nut filling make nutritious meals, providing
fibre, protein, B-group Vitamins and other minerals
and vitamins. They are convenient for packed lunches
or picnics and are delicious hot or cold.

1 Roll out the pastry and cut into
8 rounds. Place 1 tbsp (15ml)
of filling on each and fold over.

2 Seal the edges with water and
make indentations along the
seam with a fork.

3 Alternatively, pull the edges
upwards to form a spine, seal
with water and crimp the seam
with the thumb and index finger.

Black eye bean pasties (see p.91)

CIDER CASSEROLE ■

INGREDIENTS

■ 1lb (500g) potatoes,
cut into ¼ inch
(5mm) slices
■ 1 onion, finely
sliced into rings
■ 8oz (250g) sharp
eating apples, cored
and sliced
■ 3oz (75g) Cheddar
cheese, grated
■ 3 tbsp (45ml)
chopped fresh
parsley
■ ¼ pint (150ml) dry
cider

Illustrated right

This traditional combination of potatoes
and apples is enhanced here by the
addition of cider as the cooking stock.
Serve this casserole as a simple lunch dish
or as a vegetable accompaniment to a main
course.
PREPARATION TIME: 15 mins
COOKING TIME: 1–1½ hours
SERVES 4

METHOD

1 Layer the potatoes, onion, apples, most
of the cheese and the parsley in a large
casserole or ovenproof dish, reserving
some of the cheese to sprinkle on the top.
2 Pour over the cider. Sprinkle on the rest
of the cheese and cover.
3 Bake in a preheated oven at Gas Mark 5,
375°F, 190°C for 1–1½ hours until the
potatoes are tender. Serve hot.

CELERIAC WITH
■ CASHEWS ■

INGREDIENTS

■ 1lb (500g) celeriac,
chopped
■ 1lb (500g) potatoes,
chopped
■ 4 tbsp (60ml)
natural yogurt or
soured cream
■ 3 tbsp (45ml)
chopped fresh
parsley
■ ¼ tsp black pepper
■ 3oz (75g) unsalted
cashew nuts

Illustrated right

A purée of celeriac and potato, combined
here with cashew nuts, makes a nutritious
accompaniment to a bean or vegetable
casserole. If celeriac is not available, try
using swede instead.
PREPARATION TIME: 25 mins
COOKING TIME: 25 mins
SERVES 4

METHOD

1 Put the celeriac and potatoes into a large
pan. Cover with plenty of water and bring
to the boil. Simmer gently for 10–15
minutes until the vegetables are cooked.
Drain and mash well.
2 Stir in the yogurt or soured cream,
parsley, pepper and most of the cashew
nuts. Put into a casserole or ovenproof
dish and sprinkle the rest of the cashew
nuts on top.
3 Bake in a preheated oven at Gas Mark 4,
350°F, 180°C for 25 minutes until the
cashew nuts become golden brown.

TURNIPS AND PEARS
■ WITH HERBS ■

INGREDIENTS

■ 2 small turnips,
thinly sliced in rings
■ 2 pears, cored and
thinly sliced in rings
■ ½ tsp chopped
fresh marjoram
■ ½ tsp chopped
fresh basil
■ ¼ tsp black pepper
■ ¼ pint (150ml)
water
■ 1 tsp (5ml) honey
■ ½ tsp cider vinegar
■ 2 tsp (10ml)
arrowroot or
cornflour

Illustrated right

The contrast between the flavour and
texture of the turnips and pears makes this
a good accompaniment to a fairly plain
main course.
PREPARATION TIME: 10 mins
COOKING TIME: 1½ hours
SERVES 4

METHOD

1 Layer the turnips and pears in a large
casserole or ovenproof dish and sprinkle
with marjoram, basil and black pepper.
2 Mix the water, honey and cider vinegar.
Pour over the turnips and pears. Cover the
casserole and bake in a preheated oven at
Gas Mark 4, 350°F, 180°C for 1½ hours.
3 Drain off the stock from the casserole.
Mix a little of it with the arrowroot to make
a thick paste. Gradually add the rest.
4 Transfer to a small pan and bring to the
boil, stirring continuously, until the sauce
becomes thick and clear. Pour over the
turnips and pears and serve hot.

Black eye bean loaf

■ BLACK EYE BEAN LOAF ■

INGREDIENTS

■ 6oz (175g) black
eye beans, soaked, or
a 15oz (430g) can,
drained
■ 1 tbsp (15ml)
sunflower oil
■ 1 onion, finely
chopped
■ 2 cloves garlic,
crushed
■ 4oz (125g) unsalted
peanuts, chopped
■ 4oz (125g)
wholemeal
breadcrumbs
■ 2 tbsp (30ml)
tomato ketchup or
tomato purée
■ 2 tbsp (30ml) soya
sauce
■ 2 tsp (10ml)
chopped fresh basil
■ 2 tsp (10ml)
chopped fresh
marjoram
■ 2 large tomatoes,
chopped
■ 1 egg, beaten
■ 3–4 tbsp (45–60ml)
bean stock or water
and a vegetable stock
cube

Illustrated above

This loaf can also be made using red
kidney beans. Omit step 1 of the recipe if
using canned beans, but make up a small
quantity of stock for use in step 2.
PREPARATION TIME: 20 mins (plus 10–12
hours soaking time)
COOKING TIME: 40 mins (plus 40 mins for
the beans)
SERVES 4–6

METHOD

1 Drain the beans. Put in a saucepan and
cover with fresh water. Bring to the boil
and boil fast for 10 minutes. Reduce the
heat, cover and simmer for 25–30 minutes
until the beans are soft. Drain, reserving
the stock.
2 Mash the beans. Heat the oil in a pan and
gently fry the onion and garlic for 5
minutes. Mix into the mashed beans,
together with the peanuts, breadcrumbs,
tomato ketchup or purée, soya sauce, basil
and marjoram. Gently stir in the tomatoes
and the beaten egg. Add sufficient stock to
make a moist consistency.
3 Lightly oil a 1lb (500g) loaf tin. Put the
mixture into the tin and press down well.
Bake in a preheated oven at Gas Mark 4,
350°F, 180°C for 35–40 minutes. Leave in
the tin for a few minutes before turning
out. Serve hot or cold.

*CLOCKWISE FROM TOP LEFT: Turnips and pears with herbs; Celeriac with cashews;
Cider casserole*

DESSERTS

CLOCKWISE FROM TOP LEFT: *Yeasted pancakes with yogurt and fruit (see p.96); Scottish pancakes (see p.96); American-style oatmeal pancakes (see p.96)*

■ SCOTTISH PANCAKES ■

INGREDIENTS

- 4oz (125g) plain wholemeal flour
- ½ tsp bicarbonate of soda
- ½ tsp cream of tartar
- 1 egg
- 1 tbsp (15ml) clear honey
- ¼ pint (150ml) buttermilk or ordinary milk
- ½ tsp sunflower oil
- 4 tbsp (60ml) jam
- 4 tbsp (60ml) whipped cream

TO DECORATE

- 1 tsp (5ml) flaked or chopped almonds

Illustrated on page 95

Buttermilk helps to reduce the fat content of this dish but ordinary milk can be used instead.

PREPARATION TIME: 10 mins
COOKING TIME: 15 mins
MAKES: about 12 pancakes

METHOD

1 For the pancakes, put the flour, bicarbonate of soda and cream of tartar in a bowl and mix well with a whisk. In a separate bowl whisk together the egg, honey and buttermilk.
2 Heat a griddle or heavy-based frying pan over a moderate heat. Pour on the oil and wipe over with absorbent kitchen paper.
3 Pour the buttermilk mixture over the dry ingredients, stir quickly with a large spoon. Do not beat. Using 1 tbsp (15ml) batter for each pancake, cook 4 or 5 at a time. When bubbles begin to break and the surface is almost set, turn the pancakes and cook for a further 1–2 minutes.
4 Cool the pancakes, covered with a cloth, on a wire rack. Serve with 1 tsp (5ml) jam and 1 tsp (5ml) whipped cream on each pancake. Decorate with flaked or chopped almonds.

YEASTED PANCAKES WITH ■ YOGURT AND FRUIT ■

INGREDIENTS

- 1 quantity of yeasted batter (see p.65)
- 8oz (250g) Greek yogurt
- 12oz (375g) raspberries or other fresh fruit in season

Illustrated on page 95

The yeast and egg in these pancakes make them particularly light.
PREPARATION TIME: 5 mins (plus 1½ hours for the batter)
COOKING TIME: 10 mins
MAKES: about 8 pancakes

METHOD

1 Make the pancakes (see p.64). Pile the cooked pancakes on a plate and cover with a cloth to keep warm.
2 Spread the Greek yogurt over the pancakes. Decorate with the raspberries or other fresh fruit and serve immediately.

■ AMERICAN-STYLE OATMEAL ■ PANCAKES ■

INGREDIENTS

SAUCE

- 1 tsp (5ml) arrowroot or cornflour
- ¼ pint (150ml) water
- 1 tbsp (15ml) lemon juice
- 2 tbsp (30ml) clear honey
- 8oz (250g) fresh blueberries

PANCAKES

- 3oz (75g) porridge oats
- 2oz (50g) plain wholemeal flour
- 1 tsp (5ml) baking powder
- 1 egg
- 1 tbsp (15ml) sunflower oil
- 8fl oz (250ml) buttermilk or ordinary milk

Illustrated on page 95

Canned blueberries can be used for the sauce if fresh ones are out of season.
PREPARATION TIME: 15 mins (plus 10 mins for the batter)
COOKING TIME: 10 mins
MAKES: 8–10 pancakes

METHOD

1 For the sauce, put the arrowroot in a saucepan and mix to a smooth paste with 1 tsp (5ml) water. Add the remaining water, the lemon juice, honey and blueberries. Bring to the boil, stirring constantly, then reduce the heat and simmer for 10 minutes until the blueberries are tender.
2 Meanwhile, make the pancakes by mixing the oats, flour and baking powder together in a bowl.
3 Make a well in the centre and drop in the egg. Add the sunflower oil and 2 tbsp (30ml) buttermilk. Mix well, gradually adding the rest of the buttermilk and drawing in the remaining flour. Beat well.
4 Lightly grease a griddle or heavy-based frying pan. Using about 1 tbsp (15ml) batter for each pancake, cook 3 or 4 pancakes at a time over a medium heat.
5 Cook for about 2 minutes until the tops are bubbling and almost set and then turn over. Cook the other sides for 1–2 minutes. Remove and keep warm.
6 Serve the pancakes hot with the blueberry sauce and yogurt or soured cream.

■ CRÊPES SUZETTES ■

INGREDIENTS

■ 1 quantity of wholemeal batter (see p.64)
■ 3 tbsp (45ml) set honey
■ juice and grated rind 1 orange
■ 3 tbsp (45ml) Cointreau
■ 3 tbsp (45ml) brandy

TO DECORATE
■ lemon twist
■ sprig of mint

Illustrated left

The sauce for these crêpes suzettes is easy and quick to make.
PREPARATION TIME: 10 mins (plus 30 mins for the batter)
COOKING TIME: 15 mins (plus 30 mins for the pancakes)
MAKES: 8–10 pancakes

METHOD

1 Make the pancakes (see p.64). Put 1 tsp (5ml) honey on each pancake. Fold in half and half again to give a fan shape.
2 Arrange the pancakes in an ovenproof dish and pour over the orange juice. Cover with foil and heat in a preheated oven at Gas Mark 4, 350°F, 180°C for 15 minutes.
3 Put the orange rind, Cointreau and brandy in a saucepan and warm through just before serving. Remove the pancakes from the oven. Set a match to the liqueur sauce, allow to flame and pour over the pancakes or serve with a lemon twist and mint.

■ BANANA CANNELLONI ■

INGREDIENTS

■ 3oz (75g) cannelloni (about 8 tubes)
■ 4 ripe bananas
■ grated rind of 1 orange
■ 2oz (50g) fresh wholemeal breadcrumbs
■ 1 tsp (5ml) arrowroot or cornflour
■ ½ pint (300ml) orange juice
■ 2 tbsp (30ml) Cointreau

TO DECORATE
■ banana slices
■ orange rind

Illustrated left

Bananas are naturally very sweet, so resist the temptation to add sweetening.
PREPARATION TIME: 15 mins
COOKING TIME: 30 mins
SERVES 4

METHOD

1 For the filling, peel and mash the bananas, reserving some slices for decoration. Stir in most of the grated orange rind and the breadcrumbs. Fill the cannelloni with the banana mixture. Arrange in a greased ovenproof dish.
2 For the sauce, put the arrowroot into a saucepan and mix with 1 tsp (5ml) of orange juice to form a smooth paste. Add the remaining orange juice and bring to the boil, stirring constantly.
3 Remove from the heat, stir in the liqueur and pour over the cannelloni. Bake in a preheated oven at Gas Mark 6, 400°F, 200°C for 30 minutes.

CLOCKWISE FROM TOP LEFT: Banana cannelloni; Apricot flan (see p.98); Crêpes suzettes; Date and orange flan (see p.98)

■ APRICOT FLAN ■

INGREDIENTS

- ■ 4oz (125g) plain wholemeal flour
- ■ 2oz (50g) solid vegetable fat
- ■ ½ pint (300ml) water
- ■ 1 tbsp (15ml) sunflower oil
- ■ few drops almond essence
- ■ 3oz (75g) dried apricots
- ■ 8oz (250g) green grapes, deseeded and halved
- ■ ½oz (15g) flaked almonds

Illustrated on page 97

Dried apricots tend to have a better colour and flavour than fresh, but fresh apricots could be used for this filling with a little sugar added to sweeten them.

PREPARATION TIME: 45 mins (plus 1 hour 15 mins for the pastry)

COOKING TIME: 20 mins

SERVES 4

METHOD

1 For the pastry, rub the solid vegetable fat into the flour until the mixture resembles fine breadcrumbs. Stir in 2 tbsp (30ml) water, the sunflower oil and a few drops of almond essence and knead to give a fairly soft dough. Put into a polythene bag and refrigerate for 1 hour. Roll out and line a 7 inch (18cm) flan ring. Prick over the base with a fork and bake in a preheated oven at Gas Mark 6, 400°F, 200°C for 15 minutes.

2 Meanwhile, put the apricots and remaining water in a pan and bring to the boil. Reduce the heat and simmer, covered, for 30 minutes until the apricots are tender. Allow to cool and then purée.

3 Spread the apricot sauce over the base of the flan and decorate with the grapes and flaked almonds. Return to the oven for 20 minutes. Serve chilled.

■ DATE AND ORANGE FLAN ■

INGREDIENTS

BASE
- ■ 4oz (125g) plain wholemeal flour
- ■ 2oz (50g) solid vegetable fat
- ■ 2 tbsp (30ml) orange juice
- ■ 1 tbsp (15ml) sunflower oil

TOPPING
- ■ 1lb (500g) dried dates, chopped
- ■ ½ pint (300ml) orange juice
- ■ 1 orange, rind grated, peeled and segmented

TO DECORATE
- ■ orange segments
- ■ 6 lychees peeled, stoned and halved

Illustrated on page 97

Dried dates are full of fibre and vitamins. The orange juice here offsets their sticky sweetness.

PREPARATION TIME: 30 mins (plus 1 hour 15 mins for the pastry)

COOKING TIME: 20 mins

SERVES 4

METHOD

1 For the pastry, rub the solid vegetable fat into the flour until the mixture resembles fine breadcrumbs. Stir in 2 tbsp (30ml) orange juice and the sunflower oil and knead to give a fairly soft dough. Put into a polythene bag and refrigerate for 1 hour. Roll out and line a 7 inch (18cm) flan ring. Prick over the base with a fork and bake in a preheated oven at Gas Mark 6, 400°F, 200°C for 15 minutes.

2 Meanwhile, put the dates, orange juice and finely grated orange rind in a saucepan. Boil, then cover and simmer for 5 minutes. Leave to cool and then purée.

3 Fill the flan case with the date and orange purée. Decorate with orange segments and lychees. Return to the oven for 20 minutes. Serve chilled.

Fresh pear and ricotta flan

FRESH PEAR AND ■ RICOTTA FLAN ■

INGREDIENTS

PASTRY
- 4oz (125g) plain wholemeal flour
- pinch salt
- ½ tsp baking powder
- 2oz (50g) soft margarine
- 2oz (50g) soft brown sugar
- 1oz (25g) sesame seeds
- 2–3 tbsp (30–45ml) water

FILLING
- 4 pears, peeled, cored and chopped
- 7oz (200g) ricotta or curd cheese
- 3fl oz (75ml) soured cream
- 1–2 tbsp (15–30ml) maple syrup to taste
- ¼ tsp vanilla essence

TOPPING
- 1 pear
- 2 tbsp (30ml) lemon juice
- 1–2 tsp (5–10ml) agar-agar flakes (a vegetarian equivalent of gelatine)

Illustrated left

The sesame seeds and the wholemeal flour in the pastry give a good, crunchy base to the smooth fruit and cheese filling of the flan. Low-fat cheese is delicious with any fresh fruit and there is usually no need to add a sweetener, even when the fruit is cooked. The agar-agar, used for the glaze, is a vegetarian equivalent of gelatine, made from seaweed and available in powder or flake form. If you are using powder you will need less, as it is more concentrated than the flakes.

PREPARATION TIME: 1 hour (plus 30 mins resting time)

COOKING TIME: 15–20 mins

SERVES 6

METHOD

1 For the pastry, mix together the flour, salt and baking powder in a bowl.
2 Rub in the margarine until the mixture resembles fine breadcrumbs. Mix in the sugar and sesame seeds.
3 Add the water and mix to a soft dough. Leave to rest for 30 minutes.
4 Roll out and use to line a 7 inch (18cm) flan tin. Prick the base. Bake in a preheated oven at Gas Mark 6, 400°F, 200°C for 15–20 minutes. Leave to cool.
5 For the filling, purée the pears in a blender or food processor, then spread over the pastry base.
6 Mix together the ricotta or curd cheese, soured cream, maple syrup and vanilla essence in a blender. Spoon over the pear purée.
7 For the topping, thinly slice the pear, removing the core.
8 Then either lightly poach the slices of pear before arranging on the flan, or arrange the raw fruit on the flan.
9 For the glaze, make the lemon juice up to ¼ pint (150ml) with water in a saucepan. Add the agar-agar flakes and stir to dissolve. Bring to the boil and simmer for 5 minutes.
10 Brush the pears with the glaze and leave to cool. Serve cold.

Fresh cherry pashka

■ FRESH CHERRY PASHKA ■

INGREDIENTS

- 4oz (125g) cream cheese
- 6 tbsp (90ml) Greek yogurt
- 1oz (25g) butter or margarine
- 2–3 tsp (10–15ml) clear honey
- 3–4 drops vanilla essence
- 1 tbsp (15ml) raisins or sultanas
- 2 tsp (10ml) chopped nuts
- 3oz (75g) stoned cherries

Illustrated above

This is an adaptation of a traditional Russian Easter pudding. It is easy to make, looks good and will keep for about 2–3 days. For an attractive decoration add a whole walnut, a sprig of mint and some chopped nuts.

PREPARATION TIME: 20 mins (plus 12 hours standing time)

SERVES 4

METHOD

1 Mix together the cream cheese and yogurt.
2 Beat in the butter or margarine with a whisk.
3 Stir in the honey, vanilla essence, dried fruit and chopped nuts. Halve the cherries and mix in gently.
4 Pierce an 8oz (250g) carton or use a flower pot, line with muslin and stand on a plate. Spoon in the pashka. Cover and weigh down. Leave to stand for 12 hours.
5 Turn out and unwrap. Serve in small slices.

GRAPE AND PECAN
■ MERINGUE ■

INGREDIENTS

BASE
■ 3 egg whites
■ 6oz (175g) soft brown sugar

TOPPING
■ 6oz (175g) white grapes, deseeded
■ 2oz (50g) pecan nuts
■ ½ pint (300ml) Greek yogurt or thick cream

Illustrated right

The soft meringue base of this dish perfectly complements the fresh grape topping. You can deseed grapes by cutting them in half and removing the pips with the tip of a sharp knife. Pecans, probably best known because of the famous American Pecan Pie, are rather like walnuts in appearance, but have a smooth, glossy shell and a mild, sweet flavour. They also contain less fat than walnuts. For the best results, make this dessert on the day it is to be eaten.

PREPARATION TIME: 1 hour
COOKING TIME: 30 mins
SERVES 4

METHOD

1 Whisk the egg whites until stiff. Fold in the sugar.
2 Line a baking sheet with greaseproof paper or non-stick baking parchment. Spread the mixture in a 7 inch (18cm) round on the baking sheet.
3 Bake in a preheated oven at Gas Mark 4, 350°F, 180°C for 30 minutes. Cover with a cloth and leave to cool.
4 Chop the grapes and pecan nuts (reserving 8 halves for decoration). Mix with the yogurt or cream.
5 Spoon the grape mixture over the base. Decorate with the reserved pecan halves and serve immediately.

FROM TOP: Nectarine and hazelnut crunch; Grape and pecan meringue; Cherry and sunflower scone

NECTARINE AND HAZELNUT CRUNCH

INGREDIENTS

- 2oz (50g) oatmeal
- 2oz (50g) hazelnuts, coarsely chopped
- 1 tsp (5ml) grated orange rind
- 4oz (125g) butter or margarine
- 4oz (125g) wholemeal digestive biscuits, crushed
- 4 nectarines, peeled, stoned and sliced
- juice of 1 orange

Illustrated left

This is an upside-down dessert. The crunchy nut mixture keeps the fruit moist and protects it as it bakes. Try serving this dish with a good natural yogurt or soured cream.

PREPARATION TIME: 30 mins
COOKING TIME: 30 mins
SERVES 4

METHOD

1 Place the oatmeal on a baking sheet and toast in a preheated oven at Gas Mark 4, 350°F, 180°C for 8–10 minutes. Leave to cool, then mix well with the hazelnuts and orange rind.
2 Rub in the butter or margarine and mix in the crushed biscuits.
3 Lightly grease a 7 inch (18cm) flan tin. Place a layer of nectarines over the base and sprinkle with half the orange juice. Sprinkle half the nut and biscuit mixture over the top, then arrange a second layer of nectarines using the remaining slices. Sprinkle with the remaining orange juice and cover with the remaining nut and biscuit mixture.
4 Bake in a preheated oven at Gas Mark 4, 350°F, 180°C for 30 minutes. Cool, then turn out of the tin. Warm through before serving.

CHERRY AND SUNFLOWER SCONE

INGREDIENTS

SCONE BASE
- 4oz (125g) plain wholemeal flour
- 1½ tsp (7.5ml) baking powder
- ½ tsp ground cinnamon
- 1oz (25g) soft brown sugar
- 1oz (25g) sunflower seeds
- 1oz (25g) margarine
- 1 egg, beaten
- 1 tbsp (15ml) milk

TOPPING
- 1lb (500g) black cherries, stoned
- 1–2oz (25–50g) soft brown sugar
- 6fl oz (175ml) natural set yogurt

Illustrated left

This tasty scone base with a black cherry and yogurt topping is ideal for an afternoon tea.

PREPARATION TIME: 50 mins
COOKING TIME: 12 mins
SERVES 6–8

METHOD

1 For the base, stir the flour, baking powder, cinnamon, sugar and sunflower seeds together in a bowl. Rub in the margarine. Stir in the egg and the milk. Form into a soft dough.
2 Roll out to a 7 inch (18cm) round. Place on a lined baking sheet and bake in a preheated oven at Gas Mark 7, 425°F, 220°C for 12 minutes. Leave to cool.
3 For the topping, purée half the cherries in a blender or food processor until quite smooth then sweeten to taste.
4 Spread the cherry purée over the scone base. Carefully spread the yogurt on top and decorate with the remaining cherry halves.

■ LAYERED MUESLI ■

INGREDIENTS

- 1½oz (40g) walnuts, chopped
- 6oz (175g) crunchy oat cereal
- 1½oz (40g) sunflower seeds
- 2–3 bananas, peeled and sliced
- 8oz (250g) fresh dates, stoned and chopped
- ½ pint (300ml) Greek yogurt or yogurt and cream

Illustrated left

This highly nutritious pudding makes a good follow-up to a light meal. If it follows a heavier main course, the quantities given will serve 6. Serve in individual glasses.

PREPARATION TIME: 30 mins (plus 2 hours standing time)
COOKING TIME: 8–10 mins
SERVES 4

METHOD

1 Toast the walnuts for 3–4 minutes then mix with the crunchy oat cereal and sunflower seeds.
2 Arrange a layer of bananas and dates in the base of four glasses. Cover with the cereal mix, then spoon over a layer of yogurt. Continue to add layers, finishing with yogurt. Sprinkle a little cereal on top. Allow to stand for 2 hours before serving.

FROM LEFT: Bilberry trifle (see p.102); Layered muesli

■ BILBERRY TRIFLE ■

INGREDIENTS

SPONGE
■ 2 eggs
■ 2oz (50g) soft brown sugar
■ 2oz (50g) plain wholemeal flour

FILLING
■ 2 tbsp (30ml) bilberry or blackcurrant jam
■ 8oz (250g) bilberries, destalked
■ juice of 1 large orange
■ 2oz (50g) soft brown sugar

CUSTARD
■ 2 eggs
■ 1oz (25g) unbleached plain white flour
■ ¾ pint (450ml) semi-skimmed milk
■ ¼ tsp vanilla essence
■ soft brown sugar to taste

TO DECORATE
■ 1oz (25g) toasted, flaked almonds

Illustrated on page 101

This delicious trifle, flavoured with the tangy taste of bilberries, is substantial yet relatively low in fat. If bilberries are not available, try using black- or redcurrants. Top with traditional custard for a delicious dessert.

PREPARATION TIME: 50 mins
COOKING TIME: 25–30 mins
SERVES 4–6

METHOD

1 For the sponge, beat the eggs and sugar in a bowl until light and thick and the whisk leaves a trail in the mixture. Fold in the flour.
2 Spoon the mixture into a greased 6 inch (15cm) cake tin. Bake in a preheated oven at Gas Mark 4, 350°F, 180°C for 25–30 minutes.
3 Leave to cool, then slice in half to make a sandwich.
4 Fill the sponge with the jam, then chop the sponge sandwich into small pieces and put in a serving bowl or individual dishes.
5 For the filling, place the bilberries in a saucepan with the orange juice and sugar and gently simmer for 2–3 minutes. Leave to cool.
6 Spoon the berries over the sponge in each dish.
7 For the custard, whisk the eggs and flour together. Heat the milk in a saucepan and bring to the boil. Pour over the egg and flour, mixing thoroughly. Cook the mixture very slowly until the custard thickens. Add vanilla essence and sugar to taste. Spread the custard over the trifle and decorate with the almonds.

Gooseberry and banana with scones

GOOSEBERRY AND BANANA ■ WITH SCONES ■

INGREDIENTS

SCONES
■ 4oz (125g) plain wholemeal flour
■ 4oz (125g) unbleached plain white flour
■ pinch salt
■ 1 tsp (5ml) baking powder
■ 2oz (50g) soft brown sugar
■ 1½oz (40g) butter or margarine
■ 1 egg
■ 2–3fl oz (50–75ml) milk

FRUIT MIXTURE
■ 1lb (500g) gooseberries, topped and tailed
■ 4 ripe bananas, peeled and sliced
■ 1–2 tbsp (15–30ml) water
■ 2 tbsp (30ml) soft brown sugar

Illustrated above

This sweet and sharp stewed fruit combination makes an easy and delicious pudding. Gooseberries become sweet and gooey when cooked with bananas and sugar. Served with miniature scones this makes an unusual dessert.

PREPARATION TIME: 25 mins
COOKING TIME: 30 mins
SERVES 4

METHOD

1 To make the scones, mix the flours, salt, baking powder and sugar together and rub in the butter or margarine until the mixture resembles fine breadcrumbs.
2 Beat the egg and stir in the milk. Add this carefully to the flour mixture to make a soft dough. Add more milk if necessary.
3 Pat out the dough quite thinly (¼–½ inch/½–1 cm) and cut 12–16 small circles. Place on a greased baking sheet and bake for 10–12 minutes at Gas Mark 7, 425°F, 220°C.
4 Place the gooseberries and bananas in a saucepan with the water and sugar and stew for 5 minutes.
5 Serve the stewed gooseberries and bananas with the scones.

MILLET AND PEAR ■ PUDDING ■

INGREDIENTS

- 1 tbsp (15ml) sunflower oil
- 3oz (75g) millet
- ¾ pint (450ml) milk
- 3oz (75g) soft brown sugar
- 1oz (25g) sultanas
- 1 tsp(5ml) ground cinnamon
- 1 egg, separated
- 4 ripe pears, cored and sliced
- 1oz (25g) flaked almonds, toasted

Illustrated right

Millet, which is rich in protein, calcium and iron, makes a light, fluffy topping over fresh pear slices. Other fruits – pineapple and bananas or peaches and oranges, for example – would work equally well. Serve hot or cold, topped with a little yogurt.

PREPARATION TIME: 40 mins
COOKING TIME: 40 mins
SERVES 4–6

METHOD

1 Heat the oil in a large pan and gently toast the millet over a moderate heat for 5 minutes, taking care not to let it burn.
2 Add the milk, 2oz (50g) sugar, sultanas and cinnamon. Bring to the boil, cover and simmer for 20 minutes; stir occasionally to prevent it from burning. When the millet is soft and fluffy, set aside to cool slightly.
3 Stir the egg yolk into the cooled millet. In a separate bowl, whisk the egg white until stiff, then gently fold into the millet mixture.
4 Lightly oil a 1lb (500g) loaf tin or a small, deep, ovenproof dish. Mix together the pear slices, almonds and the remaining sugar. Put half of the pear mixture into the base of the tin. Cover with half of the millet mixture. Then put in the rest of the pear mixture. Top with the remaining millet.
5 Bake in a preheated oven at Gas Mark 4, 350°F, 180°C for 30–40 minutes until golden brown and firm to touch. Leave in the tin for a few minutes before turning out. Garnish the pudding with pear slices, grapes and mint, and serve hot or cold.

CLOCKWISE FROM TOP RIGHT: Millet and pear pudding; Castle fruit pudding (see p.104); Hot fruit salad (see p.104)

◼ CASTLE FRUIT PUDDING ◼

INGREDIENTS

- ◼ 6oz (175g) dried apricots (preferably Hunzas), soaked
- ◼ 2 eating apples, sliced
- ◼ ½ pint (300ml) water
- ◼ 4oz (125g) porridge oats
- ◼ 4oz (125g) plain wholemeal flour
- ◼ 2oz (50g) raisins
- ◼ 2oz (50g) blanched almonds, finely chopped
- ◼ 1oz (25g) sesame seeds
- ◼ 2 tsp (10ml) ground cinnamon
- ◼ 3oz (75g) margarine
- ◼ 3 tbsp (45ml) clear honey

TOPPING

- ◼ 2 tsp (10ml) sesame seeds

Illustrated on page 103

This crunchy baked pudding has a juicy layer of apricots and apples in the middle. Dried fruits are a good source of minerals and fibre. Other combinations could be used, such as dried dates and fresh pears, dried peaches and fresh bananas, dried figs and fresh oranges. This pudding could also be served as a cake, cut into slices.

PREPARATION TIME: 40 mins (plus overnight soaking time)

COOKING TIME: 40 mins

SERVES 6–8

METHOD

1 Put the apricots and apples into a medium pan and cover with the water. Bring to the boil, cover and simmer for 15–20 minutes until the apricots are soft. Add a little extra water during cooking if the fruit seems dry.
2 When cooked, remove and discard the stones from the apricots, if using Hunzas. Mix well with a spoon to break them up slightly. Set aside to cool.
3 Mix the oats, flour, raisins, almonds, sesame seeds and cinnamon together in a large bowl. Melt the margarine in a small pan. Pour over the oat and flour mixture. Add the honey and mix well.
4 Press half the oat mixture into the base of a 7 inch (18cm) round loose-bottomed tin. Cover with the apricots and apples. Spoon over the rest of the oat mixture, pressing down well. Sprinkle with the additional sesame seeds.
5 Bake in a preheated oven at Gas Mark 4, 350°F, 180°C for 35–40 minutes. Allow to stand in the tin for 5 minutes before serving. Serve hot or cold.

◼ HOT FRUIT SALAD ◼

INGREDIENTS

- ◼ 1 tbsp (15ml) sunflower oil
- ◼ 2 dessert apples, cut into eighths
- ◼ 2 peaches, cut into quarters
- ◼ 1 orange, peeled and segmented
- ◼ 4 plums, halved and stoned
- ◼ 1 banana, peeled and cut into chunks
- ◼ 1 tsp (5ml) ground cinnamon
- ◼ 1 tbsp (15ml) clear honey
- ◼ 3–4 drops hazelnut oil (optional)

Illustrated on page 103

Light and easy to make, this dessert is especially good when served with yogurt, smetana or soured cream. The fruits can be varied according to availability, working on the basis of 1–2 fruits per person. Melon, grapes, greengages and pears are all good substitutes.

PREPARATION TIME: 10 mins

COOKING TIME: 8 mins

SERVES 4

METHOD

1 Heat the oil in a large frying pan, saucepan or wok over a moderate heat. Add the apples and cook gently for 2–3 minutes.
2 Gradually add the peaches, orange and plums, cooking gently for 1 minute between each addition.
3 Finally add the banana and cinnamon and cook for 2 minutes. Drip the honey and hazelnut oil over the top. Serve hot or cold.

◼ SPICED EASTERN FRUITS ◼

INGREDIENTS

- ◼ 3oz (75g) dried apricots
- ◼ 3oz (75g) dried peaches
- ◼ 2oz (50g) dried figs
- ◼ 2oz (50g) sultanas
- ◼ 1½ pints (900ml) water
- ◼ 2 sachets rosehip and hibiscus tea
- ◼ 6 cloves
- ◼ 6 cardamom seeds
- ◼ clear honey to taste

TO DECORATE

- ◼ ½oz (15g) sliced pistachio nuts

Illustrated right

A compôte of dried fruit makes a wonderful staple dish, always on hand and constantly being replenished.

PREPARATION TIME: 20 mins (plus 2–3 days soaking time)

SERVES 8

METHOD

1 Chop the apricots and peaches into fine slivers.
2 Remove the hard stalk of the figs, and dice them finely.
3 Mix all the fruits together.
4 Boil the water and pour over the fruit. Add the sachets of tea, the cloves and cardamom seeds, and sweeten with honey to taste.
5 Leave covered in the fridge for at least 2 days, adding a little more water if necessary.
6 To serve, remove the spices and garnish with sliced pistachio nuts.

STIR-FRYING
▌ FRUIT ▐

*S*tir-frying is a Chinese technique for cooking vegetables in which a little oil is heated in a pan, preferably a wok (a thin round-bottomed metal pan which conducts heat well); the food is then cooked so that it retains it crispness, flavour and the maximum nutrients. Although we are familiar with the idea of stir-frying vegetables, fish and meat, it is perhaps surprising to learn that you can also stir-fry fruit. The same principles apply: use a little oil, add the slower-cooking ingredients first, cook quickly and keep the ingredients moving.

1 Heat the oil, then add the hard-fleshed fruit, leaving 1 minute between each type of fruit.

2 Gradually add the soft-fleshed fruit, ending with the softest, leaving 1 minute between each.

3 When all the fruit has been added, stir for 2 minutes. Add any seasoning as directed in the recipe you are using and serve.

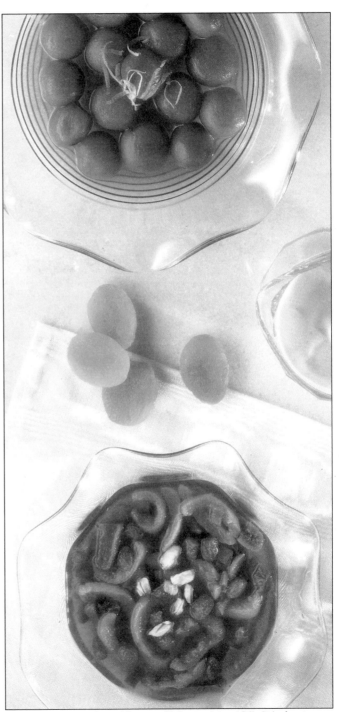

FROM TOP: Hunza apricots with sweet tahini cream (see p.106); Spiced eastern fruits

105

HUNZA APRICOTS WITH
■ SWEET TAHINI CREAM ■

INGREDIENTS

■ 10oz (300g) Hunza apricots
■ 1 tsp (5ml) clear honey

TOPPING

■ 2 tbsp (30ml) tahini
■ 3–4 tbsp (45–60ml) water
■ 3 drops vanilla essence
■ 4 tbsp (60ml) natural yogurt
■ 2–3 tsp (10–15ml) clear honey

TO DECORATE

■ finely shredded orange rind

Illustrated on page 105

Hunza or wild apricots are whole, sun-dried apricots that come complete with stone. When soaked and eaten raw, they have a sweet, subtle flavour. You can make fruit sauces from the soaking liquid, and a delicious sweetener from the stewing juice.

PREPARATION TIME: 10 mins (plus overnight soaking time)

SERVES 4

METHOD

1 Wash the apricots and soak overnight in plenty of water. Next day, drain most of the juice and keep for fruit salads.
2 Add the honey to moisten the apricots.
3 For the topping, mix the tahini thoroughly with the water until smooth. Add the remaining ingredients and mix well.
4 Pour the cream over the apricots or serve separately. Decorate with shredded orange rind.

HUNZA APRICOTS
■ WITH CALVADOS ■

INGREDIENTS

■ 8oz (250g) Hunza apricots
■ juice of 2 oranges
■ 6 cardamom seeds
■ 2 tbsp (30ml) Calvados

Illustrated right

When stewed Hunza apricots have a mellower flavour than the usual dried Turkish apricots and produce a rich juice.

PREPARATION TIME: 5 mins (plus overnight soaking time)

COOKING TIME: 30–40 mins

SERVES 4

METHOD

1 Put the fruit in a bowl with the orange juice, cover with water and soak overnight.
2 Transfer the apricots with their soaking liquid to a saucepan. Then add the cardamom seeds. Bring to the boil, cover and simmer for 30–40 minutes.
3 Add the Calvados and serve hot or cold.

FROM LEFT: Hunza apricots with Calvados; Kissel

■ KISSEL ■

INGREDIENTS

■ 4oz (125g) raspberries
■ 8oz (250g) blackberries or blackcurrants
■ 1 tsp (5ml) arrowroot or cornflour
■ 2fl oz (50ml) water
■ 4oz (125g) bilberries or blueberries
■ 1–2 tbsp (15–30ml) clear honey

Illustrated above

Kissel is a traditional Russian dish of stewed fruit, thickened with arrowroot. In this high-fibre version, I have kept some of the fruit whole for a more interesting texture. Serve it with a spoonful of natural yogurt or a little soured cream.

PREPARATION TIME: 15 mins (plus cooling time)

COOKING TIME: 5 mins

SERVES 4

METHOD

1 In a blender, purée the raspberries and half the blackberries. Sieve to remove the seeds. Place the purée in a saucepan.
2 Blend the arrowroot with 2fl oz (50ml) water, and mix into the fruit purée. Bring to the boil and simmer for 3 minutes.
3 Stir in the remaining blackberries and the bilberries. Sweeten with honey to taste. Cook on a low heat for 2 minutes to soften the whole fruits.
4 Serve cold.

STEWED GINGER PLUMS

INGREDIENTS

- 1lb (500g) cooking plums, stoned and chopped
- 2 bananas, peeled and sliced
- 4oz (125g) raisins
- ½ tsp freshly grated root ginger
- 1–2 tbsp (15–30ml) clear honey
- 2 tbsp (30ml) fruit juice (orange or apple)

Illustrated below

Raisins and bananas lend sweetness to fresh cooking plums and contribute extra vitamins and minerals. The ginger blends perfectly with the fruity taste.

PREPARATION TIME: 10 mins
COOKING TIME: 10 mins
SERVES 4

METHOD

1 Mix the plums, bananas and raisins with the grated ginger and honey. Add the fruit juice.
2 Cover and gently stew the fruit over a very low heat for 10 minutes or until just softened.
3 Serve hot or warm.

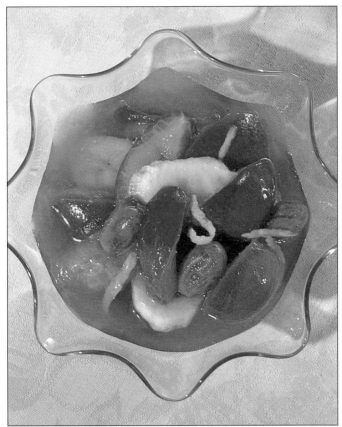

Stewed ginger plums

MAKING A ■ PINEAPPLE CASE ■

A scooped-out pineapple makes an attractive and exotic-looking case for a tropical-style fruit salad. As well as the fresh colour and interesting shape, it makes a sturdy and generous container. Oranges and lemons also make attractive cases, usually for sorbets and ice creams, and can be prepared in the same way as pineapple. To harden the cases before filling, leave in the fridge overnight.

1 *Working from the leaf end, cut the pineapple in half lengthways with a sharp knife.*

2 *Score carefully around the side with a knife leaving a broad casing and scoop out the flesh with a knife and spoon.*

3 *Alternatively, cut a lid off the pineapple and scoop out the flesh in the same way.*

■ SESAME FRUITS ■

INGREDIENTS

■ 4 medium oranges, peeled and thinly sliced into rings
■ 2 tart eating apples, cored and thinly sliced into rings
■ 2 tbsp (30ml) tahini
■ 2 tbsp (30ml) clear honey
■ ¼ pint (150ml) orange juice
■ 1 tbsp (15ml) sesame seeds

Illustrated right

When tahini, a sesame seed paste, is mixed with honey it makes a good sweet sauce for a layer of thinly sliced oranges and apples.

PREPARATION TIME: 10 mins
COOKING TIME: 30 mins
SERVES 4

METHOD

1 Layer the orange and apple slices in a casserole or ovenproof dish.
2 Mix together the tahini and honey to form a smooth paste. Add the orange juice gradually, stirring to form a smooth sauce. Pour over the fruits.
3 Sprinkle over the sesame seeds. Cover the casserole or dish.
4 Bake in a preheated oven at Gas Mark 4, 350°F, 180°C for 30 minutes. Serve hot or cold.

■ CRISP PEACHES ■

INGREDIENTS

■ 4 peaches
■ 3oz (75g) hazelnuts, coarsely ground
■ 1 tbsp (15ml) ground cinnamon
■ 1 tbsp (15ml) clear honey
■ 1oz (25g) butter or margarine
■ 3–4 tbsp (45–60ml) water

Illustrated right

Served hot or cold with natural yogurt, soured cream or fromage frais, this versatile recipe makes a luxurious dessert. Pears could be used when peaches are unavailable.

PREPARATION TIME: 15 mins
COOKING TIME: 20–25 mins
SERVES 4

METHOD

1 Halve and stone the peaches. Put into the base of a large casserole or ovenproof dish with the cut sides uppermost.
2 Combine the hazelnuts and cinnamon in a small bowl. Melt the honey and butter or margarine over a moderate heat in a small pan. Pour over the hazelnuts and cinnamon and mix well.
3 Top each of the peach halves with some of the nut mixture. Spoon the water around the peaches and cover the dish.
4 Bake in a preheated oven at Gas Mark 4, 350°F, 180°C for 20 minutes. If desired, the peaches can be browned under a preheated moderate grill for 5 minutes before serving. Serve hot or cold.

FROM TOP: Sesame fruits; Crisp peaches; Spiced nectarines

■ SPICED NECTARINES ■

INGREDIENTS

■ 3oz (75g) butter or margarine
■ 6oz (175g) wholemeal breadcrumbs
■ 1 tbsp (15ml) clear honey
■ 1 tbsp (15ml) soft brown sugar
■ 2oz (50g) blanched almonds, finely chopped
■ 4 nectarines, halved and stoned
■ ½ pint (300ml) apple juice
■ 1 tsp (5ml) ground cinnamon
■ ½ teaspoon grated nutmeg
■ 2 cloves

Illustrated left

Nectarines or peaches cooked gently in spices and apple juice are delicious hot or cold with Greek yogurt.

PREPARATION TIME: 15 mins
COOKING TIME: 25 mins
SERVES 4

METHOD

1 Melt the butter or margarine in a pan. Add the breadcrumbs, honey, sugar and almonds. Cook over a moderate heat for 10 minutes, stirring occasionally. Divide the mixture between 4 individual dishes.
2 Put the nectarines, apple juice, cinnamon, nutmeg and cloves into a pan. Bring to the boil, reduce the heat and simmer gently for 10 minutes, until the fruit is just soft. Put 2 nectarine halves on top of the breadcrumb mixture in each dish.
3 Bring the remaining juice up to the boil and boil rapidly for 2–3 minutes to reduce the liquid. Remove the cloves and pour a little juice over each dish.

FROM TOP: Madeira and orange syllabub; Apricot and almond fool

■ APRICOT AND ■ ALMOND FOOL ■

INGREDIENTS

■ 1lb (500g) fresh apricots, halved and stoned, or 8oz (250g) dried apricots
■ ½ pint (300ml) natural yogurt
■ 1–2oz (25–50g) almond pieces
■ 2 tsp (10ml) clear honey
■ ½ tsp vanilla essence

Illustrated right

Nut creams make a delicious base for fools or creamy desserts.

PREPARATION TIME: 15 mins (plus chilling time)
COOKING TIME: about 10 mins
SERVES 4

METHOD

1 Reserve 4 apricots, then place the rest in a pan. Simmer in a little water until soft. Purée until smooth and leave to cool. When the purée is cold, fold in the yogurt.
2 Grind the almonds finely in a food processor or grinder. Add enough water to make a thick cream. Sweeten with honey and add vanilla essence. Add the apricot purée and blend until quite smooth. Spoon into 4 individual glasses, decorate with the reserved apricots and serve chilled.

■ MADEIRA AND ■ ORANGE SYLLABUB ■

INGREDIENTS

■ 2 oranges, peeled, segmented and chopped
■ 3–4 tbsp (45–60ml) Madeira
■ 3–4fl oz (75–125ml) soured cream or smetana
■ 3oz (75g) cream cheese
■ 2oz (50g) soft brown sugar
■ 1 tsp (5ml) grated orange rind
■ 2 tbsp (30ml) orange juice
■ 2 egg whites or a quantity of dried egg white

Illustrated above

A deliciously rich syllabub. Use grape juice for a non-alcoholic alternative. Dried egg white may be used.

PREPARATION TIME: 15 mins (plus chilling time)
SERVES 4

METHOD

1 Place the chopped oranges in a bowl. Sprinkle with 1 tbsp (15ml) Madeira. Chill.
2 Whisk together the soured cream, cream cheese, sugar, remaining Madeira, orange rind and juice until quite smooth.
3 Whisk the egg whites until stiff. Fold into the syllabub mixture and chill.
4 Before serving, spoon a portion of chopped orange into each dish and cover with syllabub.

▌ BILBERRY MOUSSE ▌

INGREDIENTS

- ▌ 12oz (375g) bilberries
- ▌ 2oz (50g) soft brown sugar
- ▌ 4 tbsp (60ml) water
- ▌ 2 tsp (10ml) arrowroot or cornflour
- ▌ 4 cloves
- ▌ 6–8 tbsp (90–120ml) Greek yogurt
- ▌ 1 egg white or a quantity of dried egg white

Illustrated left

This delicious, light mousse can be made equally well with blackcurrants, blackberries or tayberries, if bilberries prove difficult to find. Greek yogurt or soured cream on top gives the finishing touch. Dried egg may be used.

PREPARATION TIME: 30 mins (plus chilling time)
SERVES 4

METHOD

1 Wash the bilberries. Place in a saucepan with the sugar and water and poach for 2–3 minutes until the juices run. Purée well in a blender. Sieve, then return to the pan.
2 Dissolve the arrowroot in a little water and add to the bilberry purée. Bring to the boil with the cloves, then simmer for 3–4 minutes, stirring. Remove the cloves. Cool.
3 When cold, stir in the yogurt.
4 Whisk the egg white until stiff and fold in. Pile into individual glasses and chill before serving. Serve with yogurt or soured cream.

BANANA AND MANGO ▌ FOOL ▌

INGREDIENTS

- ▌ 1 large mango
- ▌ 5oz (150g) fromage frais
- ▌ 1 banana, peeled

Illustrated right

To be sure the dish does not discolour, prepare it only about half an hour before serving. Choose a ripe mango with golden skin; if it is still a little green, leave to ripen in a warm room.

PREPARATION TIME: 10 mins (plus chilling time)
SERVES 4

METHOD

1 Peel the mango and cut the flesh away from the stone, reserving a few slices for decoration.
2 In a blender or food processor, mix the fromage frais, mango and banana together until smooth.
3 Spoon into 4 dessert dishes and decorate with the reserved slices of mango. Chill before serving.

APPLE AND ■ GOOSEBERRY FOOL ■

INGREDIENTS

■ 1lb (500g) gooseberries, topped and tailed
■ 2 cooking apples, about 10oz (300g), peeled, cored and thinly sliced
■ ½ tsp vanilla essence
■ 1–2 tbsp (15–30ml) clear honey (or to taste)
■ 1 tbsp (15ml) water
■ 8oz (250g) curd cheese or cream cheese
■ 7fl oz (200ml) Greek yogurt

Illustrated left

Yogurt and curd or cream cheese combine to make a delicious base for a fruit fool. For the best texture, leave in the gooseberry pips and skin – this will also add to the overall fibre content.

PREPARATION TIME: 20 mins (plus chilling time)

COOKING TIME: 10 mins

SERVES 6

METHOD

1 Place the gooseberries and apple slices in a small saucepan, reserving a few slivers of apple for decoration. Add the vanilla essence, honey and water.
2 Cover and cook very gently for about 10 minutes or until the mixture has reduced to a pulp.
3 Allow to cool slightly, then beat in the curd or cream cheese and yogurt.
4 Taste for sweetness and add more honey if necessary. Serve chilled with the slivers of apple on top.

CLOCKWISE FROM TOP: Banana and mango fool; Passion fruit praline; Yuletide soufflé (see p.112)

■ PASSION FRUIT PRALINE ■

INGREDIENTS

PRALINE
■ 2oz (50g) hazelnuts
■ 2oz (50g) dark brown sugar

BASE
■ 8 passion fruit
■ 1 tbsp (15ml) orange juice
■ 4oz (125g) soft brown sugar
■ 6oz (175g) cream cheese
■ 2 eggs, beaten

Illustrated left

This passion-fruit-flavoured base transforms into an "egg custard" when baked and blends deliciously with the caramelized hazelnuts (praline). The subtle colouring and flavour of the passion fruit is mouthwatering, but this dish will work equally well with 4 mangoes or 6 peaches.

PREPARATION TIME: 30 mins

COOKING TIME: 20 mins

SERVES 4–6

METHOD

1 For the praline, toast the hazelnuts under a preheated grill for 2–3 minutes. Then rub the skins off with a clean cloth.
2 In a pan, mix the nuts and sugar together and heat gently until the sugar dissolves.
3 Raise the heat and boil the mixture for 5–10 minutes or until the nuts pop.
4 Pour the mixture on to a greased baking sheet and allow to cool. When cold, crush in a food processor or grinder, or place between two sheets of greaseproof paper and roll over firmly with a rolling pin.
5 For the base, scoop out the flesh and seeds from the passion fruit and place in a saucepan with the orange juice and sugar.
6 Simmer for 2–3 minutes. Strain, sieving out as many seeds as possible. Leave to cool.
7 Mix the passion fruit flesh with the cream cheese and eggs.
8 Divide the mixture between 4–6 ramekin dishes. Top each with the praline mixture.
9 Bake in a preheated oven at Gas Mark 4, 350°F, 180°C for 15–20 minutes or until just set. Serve warm.

∎ YULETIDE SOUFFLÉ ∎

INGREDIENTS

- 4oz (125g) pitted prunes
- 4oz (125g) raisins
- ¼ pint (150ml) water
- juice of ½ orange
- 2 tbsp (30ml) clear honey
- 1 tbsp (15ml) brandy
- ¼ tsp vanilla essence
- 3 eggs, separated

Illustrated on page 111

Christmas is traditionally the time not only of good cheer and hospitality, but also of stodgy food, plenty of alcohol, and endless sweets, chocolates and mince pies. Not surprisingly, many people find they simply cannot manage that rich, heavy wedge of Christmas pudding. This gorgeous light dessert makes a good alternative. It does not use sugar and is low in fat. Dried fruits and orange juice contribute vitamins and minerals and lend a sweet, rich taste to the dish.

PREPARATION TIME: 40 mins (plus overnight soaking time)
COOKING TIME: 25–30 mins
SERVES 4

METHOD

1 Soak the prunes and raisins overnight in the water and orange juice and honey.
2 Gently simmer the prune and raisin mixture for 10 minutes or until soft.
3 In a blender or food processor, purée the fruits, using a little of the cooking liquid to form a soft paste.
4 Blend in the brandy, vanilla essence and egg yolks.
5 Whisk the egg whites until stiff then fold into the blended mixture.
6 Wrap a length of greaseproof paper around the top of a small soufflé dish, so that about 1 inch (2.5cm) overlaps the rim, and secure with string or tape.
7 Spoon the mixture into the bowl. Bake in a preheated oven at Gas Mark 5, 375°F, 190°C for 25–30 minutes until well risen and fairly firm. Remove the paper collar and serve immediately.

FROM TOP: Grapefruit sorbet; Mango and pineapple parfait

∎ GRAPEFRUIT SORBET ∎

INGREDIENTS

- 4oz (125g) soft brown sugar
- ¼ pint (150ml) water
- 1 large grapefruit
- 2 egg whites or a quantity of dried egg white

Illustrated above

Fruit sorbets can be made from almost any fruit but the tang of grapefruit goes particularly well with the sweet syrup. Dried egg white may be used.

PREPARATION TIME: 15 mins (plus 2–3 hours cooling and freezing time)
SERVES 4

METHOD

1 Bring the sugar and water to the boil, and boil hard for 5 minutes to make a light syrup. Leave to cool.
2 Peel the grapefruit and blend the flesh in a blender or food processor until smooth.
3 Mix the puréed grapefruit with the sugar syrup and egg whites. Freeze for 30 minutes, then turn into a large chilled bowl and beat for 4–5 minutes. Freeze again for 2 hours. Allow the sorbet to defrost slightly before serving.

MANGO AND
■ PINEAPPLE PARFAIT ■

INGREDIENTS

■ 7 fl oz (200ml)
natural set yogurt
■ 1–2 tbsp (15–30ml)
clear honey
■ 8oz (250g) mango
flesh, chopped
■ 8oz (250g) fresh
pineapple flesh,
chopped
■ 8oz (250g)
strawberries, hulled
(optional)

Illustrated left

Yogurt ice cream is delicious, healthy and easy to make. Try to make it on the day it is to be eaten, however, or it may become hard and icy.

PREPARATION TIME: 15 mins (plus 2–3 hours freezing time)
SERVES 4

METHOD

1 Mix together the yogurt and honey. Place in a shallow freezerproof container and freeze until just firm.
2 Transfer to a blender or food processor and mix well.
3 Mix the chopped mango and pineapple together. Add to the yogurt and blend.
4 Return the mixture to the container and freeze for 2 hours or until firm. Scoop out and serve alone or with strawberries.

■ PASSION FRUIT SAUCE ■

INGREDIENTS

■ 6 passion fruit
■ 3 large oranges
■ 1–2oz (25–50g) soft
brown sugar
■ ½ tsp arrowroot or
cornflour

Illustrated right

The glorious colour and flavour of this fruit sauce make it ideal for special occasions. Use it on pancakes or yogurt ice creams.

PREPARATION TIME: 20 mins
MAKES: 7 fl oz (200ml)

METHOD

1 Halve the passion fruit and scoop out the flesh.
2 Halve and squeeze the oranges, then mix the juice and the sugar with the passion fruit flesh in a saucepan. Heat the mixture gently for 3–4 minutes.
3 Sieve the juice to remove the passion fruit seeds.
4 Dissolve the arrowroot in a little water and mix into the fruit juice. Bring to the boil, cover and simmer for 3 minutes. Serve hot or cold.

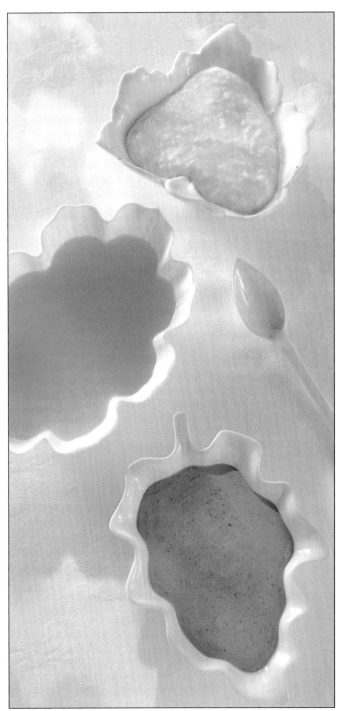

FROM TOP: Apple and yogurt sauce (see p.114); Passion fruit sauce; Curd cheese and damson sauce (see p.114)

CURD CHEESE AND
■ DAMSON SAUCE ■

INGREDIENTS

■ 12oz (375g)
damsons or plums,
stoned and chopped
■ 1–2 tbsp (15–30ml)
water
■ 1–2 tbsp (15–30ml)
soft brown sugar
■ 4oz (125g) curd
cheese
■ 2 tbsp (30ml)
brandy (optional)

Illustrated on page 113

Made from semi-skimmed milk, curd
cheese has a medium-fat content and is
denser than most other soft cheeses. Here
it enriches the sauce, making it smooth and
creamy, yet much lighter than a roux-based
version. Use the sauce over fruit, ice cream
or a pancake base.
PREPARATION TIME: 15 mins
MAKES: ¾ pint (450ml)

METHOD

1 Place the damsons with the water and
sugar in a saucepan. Cook them for
10 minutes or until just soft.
2 Purée in a blender or sieve until smooth.
3 Add the cheese and brandy (if using)
and blend again.
4 Warm over a low heat and serve.

APPLE AND YOGURT
■ SAUCE ■

INGREDIENTS

■ 3 cooking apples,
peeled, cored and
diced
■ 3 tbsp (45ml) clear
honey
■ 3 tbsp (45ml) water
■ 7fl oz (200ml)
natural yogurt
■ 1 tsp (5ml)
cornflour

Illustrated on page 113

Yogurt adds a sharp flavour and helps to
lighten this fruit sauce, which is delicious
over muesli, fruit or a biscuit base. It makes
a healthy alternative to cream, and an easy
way to eke out cottage cheese or skimmed
milk soft cheese (quark). It is, of course,
very tasty on its own, with perhaps a little
honey. When heating yogurt, add
cornflour to prevent it separating.
PREPARATION TIME: 20 mins
COOKING TIME: 10 mins
MAKES: ½ pint (300ml)

METHOD

1 Place the apples with the honey and
water in a saucepan. Stew gently until
tender. Purée in a blender until the
mixture is smooth.
2 Mix the yogurt with the cornflour. Add
to the apple purée.
3 Simmer gently for 5 minutes to heat
through and cook the cornflour, stirring
constantly. Serve warm.

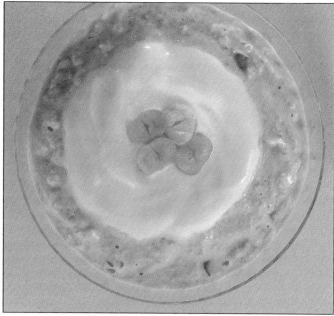

Apple and hazelnut cream

APPLE AND
■ HAZELNUT CREAM ■

INGREDIENTS

■ 2oz (50g) porridge
oats
■ 2–3 tbsp (30–45ml)
clear honey
■ 8fl oz (250ml) cold
water
■ 2oz (50g) hazelnuts
■ 4 dessert apples,
cored
■ juice of ½ orange
■ 2 tsp (10ml) grated
orange rind
■ 7fl oz (200ml)
natural yogurt

TOPPING
■ ¼ pint (150ml)
natural yogurt

TO DECORATE
■ 1 tbsp (15ml)
hazelnuts, toasted
and sliced

Illustrated above

This smooth, rich-tasting dessert is based
on the original muesli recipe. For the best
flavour, grate the apple very finely and
serve with extra yogurt.
PREPARATION TIME: 15 mins (plus 2 hours
soaking and chilling time)
SERVES 4

METHOD

1 Soak the oats in the honey and water for
at least 2 hours.
2 Toast the hazelnuts lightly under a
preheated grill for 3–4 minutes. Cool, then
chop very finely.
3 Finely grate the apples, including the
skin. Mix with the soaked oats and
remaining ingredients.
4 Divide into individual glasses, top with
yogurt, refrigerate and serve chilled,
decorated with hazelnut slices.

CLOCKWISE FROM TOP: *Tropical cocktail; Summer fruit cup; Banana yogurt drink*

▐ TROPICAL COCKTAIL ▐

INGREDIENTS

- 4oz (125g) seedless grapes
- 8oz (250g) pineapple, chopped
- 8oz (250g) watermelon, chopped
- clear honey to taste

Illustrated left

This makes a deliciously refreshing drink. Instead of diluting the fruit pulp with water, try adding sparkling mineral water to make a fizzy drink.

PREPARATION TIME: 10 mins
MAKES: 1 pint (600ml)

METHOD

1 Wash the grapes. Purée thoroughly with the other fruit in a blender or food processor.
2 Sieve to remove the fibrous flesh.
3 Dilute and sweeten with honey to taste.

▐ SUMMER FRUIT CUP ▐

INGREDIENTS

- 4oz (125g) strawberries
- 4oz (125g) raspberries
- 8fl oz (250ml) red grape juice
- clear honey to taste

Illustrated left

Home-made cocktails can be easily made in a blender or food processor, without investing in a juicer. This makes a fairly concentrated mixture, so you may need to add quite a lot of water to dilute it to drinking consistency.

PREPARATION TIME: 10 mins
MAKES: 17fl oz (500ml)

METHOD

1 Hull the strawberries and raspberries, then purée in a blender or food processor until smooth.
2 Sieve the mixture to remove the pips.
3 Mix with the grape juice, dilute to taste, and sweeten with honey to taste.

▐ BANANA YOGURT DRINK ▐

INGREDIENTS

- 1 large banana, peeled
- juice of 1 large orange
- 2 tbsp (30ml) lemon juice
- 4–8fl oz (125–250ml) thin natural yogurt
- clear honey to taste

Illustrated left

This nutritious smooth drink is delicious fresh from the fridge, but extra special with a little rum added.

PREPARATION TIME: 10 mins
MAKES: 8–10fl oz (250–300ml)

METHOD

1 Purée the banana and fruit juices together in a blender or food processor.
2 Dilute to drinking consistency with the yogurt and sweeten to taste.

❚ BREADS ❚

CLOCKWISE FROM TOP LEFT: *Soda bread (see p.119); Rice bread (see p.119); Basic wholemeal rolls (see p.118)*

BASIC WHOLEMEAL
■ BREAD ■

INGREDIENTS

- 1oz (25g) fresh yeast
- 2 tsp (10ml) soft brown sugar
- ¾ pint (450ml) warm water
- 1½lb (750g) plain wholemeal flour
- 1 tsp (5ml) salt
- 1 tbsp (15ml) sunflower oil

Illustrated below

Quick and simple, this recipe makes a delicious bread and can be used as the basis for many variations.

PREPARATION TIME: 1½ hours
COOKING TIME: 35–40 mins
MAKES: two 1lb (500g) loaves or one 2¼lb (1kg) loaf approx

METHOD

1 Cream the yeast and sugar together. Pour on ¼ pint (150ml) of the warm water and mix well.
2 Mix the flour with the salt in a warm dry bowl. Pour the yeast mixture over the flour. Add the remaining water and the oil. Stir with a wooden spoon until the dough starts to form. Knead well for up to 10 minutes until the dough becomes smooth.
3 Transfer to a clean bowl, cover with oiled clingfilm and leave the dough to rise in a warm place for about 1 hour until it has doubled in size.
4 Take the dough out of the bowl and knead again for a few minutes. Divide the dough in half and shape into loaves. Place in two greased 1lb (500g) loaf tins, or shape the dough into one large loaf and place in a greased 2lb (1kg) loaf tin. Leave to prove for 15–20 minutes or until well risen.
5 Bake in a preheated oven at Gas Mark 7, 425°F, 220°C for 35–40 minutes (20 mins for rolls). The bread is done if it sounds hollow when tapped on the base. Cool on a wire rack.

Basic wholemeal bread

BASIC
■ WHOLEMEAL BREAD ■

*I*t takes less time to make bread than you might think, because most of the preparation time is in fact the rising and proving time. The delicious smell and nutty texture of freshly baked, homemade, wholemeal bread make it well worth the effort. You can always shape the dough into rolls instead of a loaf for variety.

1 Mix the flour and salt. Pour on the yeast mixture. Add the remaining water and oil and stir into a dough.

2 Knead the dough for 10 mins. Transfer to a clean bowl. Cover with oiled clingfilm and leave to rise for 1 hour.

3 Knead the dough briefly. Mould the dough into a loaf or rolls.

■ SODA BREAD ■

INGREDIENTS

■ 1lb (500g) plain wholemeal flour
■ 1 tsp (5ml) bicarbonate of soda
■ 2 tsp (10ml) salt
■ ½ pint (300ml) buttermilk or ordinary milk

Illustrated on page 117

This soda bread is very quick to make and is best eaten warm. It is important to bake the bread immediately the dough is mixed, as the bicarbonate of soda starts to act as soon as it is wet.

PREPARATION TIME: 15 mins
COOKING TIME: 45–50 mins
MAKES: one large 1½lb (750g) cob or two small ¾lb (375g) cobs approx

METHOD

1 Sift the flour with the soda and salt into a bowl. Pour in the buttermilk and mix to a soft dough. Add a little warm water if necessary.
2 Shape into one large cob or two small ones. Mark a cross in the top of each. Place on a greased and floured baking sheet.
3 Bake in a preheated oven at Gas Mark 7, 425°F, 220°C for 30 minutes, then reduce the oven temperature to Gas Mark 6, 400°F, 200°C and bake for a further 15–20 minutes. Cool on a wire rack.

■ RICE BREAD ■

INGREDIENTS

■ 2oz (50g) uncooked brown rice and ½ pint (300ml) water for cooking (or 5–6oz/150–175g cooked brown rice)
■ ½oz (15g) fresh yeast
■ 1 tsp (5ml) soft brown sugar
■ ½ pint (300ml) warm water
■ 1lb (500g) plain wholemeal flour
■ 1 tsp (5ml) salt
■ 1 tbsp (15ml) oil

Illustrated on page 117

Cooked grains, especially rice, add moisture and texture to a plain wholemeal dough. They make the loaf stay fresh for longer, and contribute extra fibre.

PREPARATION TIME: 1½–2 hours
COOKING TIME: 35–40 mins (plus 20–25 mins for the rice)
MAKES: approx one 1½lb (625g) loaf

METHOD

1 Cook the rice in ½ pint (300ml) boiling water for 20–25 minutes until tender. Drain well and set aside.
2 Cream the yeast and sugar and mix in ¼ pint (150ml) warm water.
3 Mix the flour and salt. Pour over the yeast mixture. Add the remaining ¼ pint (150ml) warm water and the oil to the yeast and flour mixture. Knead well, adding more flour or liquid to make a soft dough.
4 Put the dough into a clean bowl and cover with oiled clingfilm or a damp cloth and leave for 45–60 minutes, or until well risen.
5 Knead again and work in the cooked rice. Shape into a loaf and place into a well-oiled loaf tin. Cover with oiled clingfilm or a damp cloth and leave for 30 minutes then bake at Gas Mark 7, 425°F, 220°C for 35–40 minutes. Cool on a wire rack.

Batter method wholemeal bread

BATTER METHOD
▌ WHOLEMEAL BREAD ▌

INGREDIENTS

▪ 1oz (25g) fresh yeast
▪ 2 tsp (10ml) soft brown sugar
▪ ¾ pint (450ml) warm water
▪ 1½lb (750g) plain wholemeal flour
▪ 1 tsp (5ml) salt
▪ 1 tbsp (15ml) sunflower oil

Illustrated above

This technique is useful when using a mixture of high-gluten and low-gluten flours (such as rye or buckwheat), and for unsweetened breads.

PREPARATION TIME: 1½ hours
COOKING TIME: 25–35 mins
MAKES: one 2¼lb (1kg) loaf or two 1lb (500g) loaves approx

METHOD

1 Cream the yeast and sugar and pour over the warm water. Stir in half the flour and mix to a batter. Cover with oiled clingfilm or a damp cloth and leave for 30 minutes. Add the remaining flour, salt and oil. Work to a dough and knead.
2 Transfer to a clean bowl, cover with oiled clingfilm or a damp cloth and leave to prove for 45–60 minutes.
3 Knead again briefly then shape the dough into one or two loaves. Place in a greased 2lb (1kg) loaf tin or two 1lb (500g) tins. Cover and leave to prove for 20–30 minutes, or until well risen. Bake in a pre-heated oven at Gas Mark 7, 425°F, 220°C for 25–35 minutes. Cool on a wire rack.

Honey and almond bread

HONEY AND ALMOND
▌ BREAD ▌

INGREDIENTS

▪ 1oz (25g) fresh yeast
▪ 1 tbsp (15ml) clear honey
▪ ½ pint (300ml) warm milk
▪ 1lb (500g) plain wholemeal flour
▪ ½ tsp salt
▪ 2oz (50g) ground almonds
▪ 1oz (25g) butter
▪ 1 egg, beaten

Illustrated above

This is a delicious light bread made with an enriched dough flavoured with almonds. Serve it at tea time or for a special breakfast.

PREPARATION TIME: 2 hours
COOKING TIME: 30–35 mins
MAKES: approx one 2lb (1kg) loaf or two 1lb (500g) loaves

METHOD

1 Cream the yeast with the honey, milk and 4oz (125g) flour. Beat until smooth. Cover with oiled clingfilm or a damp cloth and leave for 30 minutes, or until frothy.
2 In a separate bowl mix the remaining flour, salt and almonds. Rub in the butter. Pour on the yeast mixture and add the beaten egg, then knead well. Put in a clean bowl, cover with oiled clingfilm or a damp cloth and leave for 45–60 minutes, or until well risen.
3 Knead again, then shape into a loaf and put into a well-oiled 2lb (1kg) loaf tin or two 1lb (500g) tins. Cover with oiled clingfilm or a damp cloth and leave for 30 minutes then bake at Gas Mark 7, 425°F, 220°C for 30–35 minutes. Cool on a wire rack.

■ GRANARY® COB ■

INGREDIENTS

- ■ ½oz (15g) fresh yeast
- ■ 2 tbsp (30ml) malt extract
- ■ 8–10fl oz (250–300ml) warm water
- ■ 8oz (250g) plain wholemeal flour
- ■ 8oz (250g) granary-type flour
- ■ 1 tsp (5ml) salt
- ■ 1 tbsp (15ml) sunflower oil

GARNISH

- ■ 1–2 tbsp (15–30ml) kibbled or cracked wheat

Illustrated below

Granary-type flour is a wheatmeal flour containing some malted whole wheat grains. Granary bread is a healthy, versatile loaf.

PREPARATION TIME: 1½ hours
COOKING TIME: 25–35 mins
MAKES: approx one 1½lb (750g) cob

METHOD

1 Cream the yeast and malt extract and mix in about half the water.

2 Mix the flours and salt in a bowl. Add the yeast mixture, the remaining water and the oil. Knead well. Transfer to a clean bowl. Cover with oiled clingfilm or a damp cloth and leave to rise for 30 minutes or until double in size. Knead, shape into a cob, then dip in cracked wheat. Place on a greased baking sheet. Cover and leave for 20–30 minutes.

3 Bake in a preheated oven at Gas Mark 7, 425°F, 220°C for 25–35 minutes. Cool on a wire rack.

Unbleached white plaited ring

UNBLEACHED WHITE ■ PLAITED RING ■

INGREDIENTS

- ■ 1oz (25g) fresh yeast
- ■ 1 tbsp (15ml) clear honey
- ■ ¾ pint (450ml) warm water
- ■ 1½lb (750g) unbleached plain white flour
- ■ 1 tsp (5ml) salt
- ■ 1 tbsp (15ml) sunflower oil

GLAZE (optional)

- ■ a little beaten egg

Illustrated above

After using wholemeal flour, white dough feels pliable, easy to handle and rises well. It can taste bland, so if you want white bread to complement a light soup or summer salad, choose a good quality unbleached white flour, and add a little oil to improve the dough.

PREPARATION TIME: 1½ hours
COOKING TIME: 25–30 mins
MAKES: approx one 2½lb (1.2kg) loaf

METHOD

1 Cream the yeast with the honey and stir in ¼ pint (150ml) warm water.

2 Mix the flour with the salt in a bowl. Pour over the yeast mixture, the remaining warm water and the sunflower oil and knead well, adding more flour or liquid if necessary. Transfer to a clean bowl. Cover with oiled clingfilm or a damp cloth and leave for 30–40 minutes or until well risen.

3 Knead again briefly. Divide the dough into three pieces. Roll each piece into a very long rope. Plait the pieces together, then fold the ends of the plait in towards the centre to make a 'B' shape. Place on a greased baking sheet. Cover with oiled clingfilm or a damp cloth and leave to prove for 20–25 minutes or until well risen. Brush with egg.

4 Bake in a preheated oven at Gas Mark 7, 425°F, 220°C for 25–30 minutes. Cool on a wire rack.

Granary® cob

ENRICHED WHOLEMEAL
■ BREAD WITH POPPY SEEDS ■

INGREDIENTS

- ■ ¾oz (20g) fresh yeast
- ■ 1 tbsp (15ml) clear honey
- ■ ½ pint (300ml) warm water
- ■ 1lb (500g) plain wholemeal flour
- ■ 1 tsp (5ml) salt
- ■ 2 tbsp (30ml) skimmed milk powder
- ■ 2 tbsp (30ml) wheatgerm
- ■ 2 tbsp (30ml) ground almonds
- ■ 2 tbsp (30ml) porridge oats
- ■ 1 tbsp (15ml) sunflower oil

GARNISH

- ■ a little beaten egg
- ■ 1–2 tbsp (15–30ml) poppy seeds

Illustrated below

There are many ways to enrich a basic dough – skimmed milk powder, nuts, seeds, as well as flakes and flours. This recipe produces a nutty-tasting loaf with a dry crumb.

PREPARATION TIME: 1½ hours

COOKING TIME: 25–35 mins

MAKES: approx two 1lb (500g) loaves

METHOD

1 Cream the yeast and honey and mix in 3–4 tbsp (45–60ml) warm water.

2 Mix the flour with the salt, milk powder, wheatgerm, ground almonds and porridge oats. Stir in the yeast mixture, the oil and the remaining water. Knead well, adding more flour or liquid if necessary. Transfer to a clean bowl. Cover with oiled clingfilm or a damp cloth and leave for 35–40 minutes or until well risen.

3 Knead again lightly. Divide the dough in half and shape into loaves. Place in two lightly greased 1lb (500g) loaf tins. Cover with oiled clingfilm or a damp cloth and leave to prove for 20 minutes or until well risen. Brush with beaten egg and sprinkle with poppy seeds. Bake in a preheated oven at Gas Mark 7, 425°F, 220°C for 25–35 minutes. Cool on wire racks.

Enriched wholemeal bread with poppy seeds

Herb bread in a flower pot

HERB BREAD
■ IN A FLOWER POT ■

INGREDIENTS

- ■ ½oz (15g) fresh yeast
- ■ 1 tsp (5ml) soft brown sugar
- ■ ½ pint (300ml) warm water
- ■ 1lb (500g) plain wholemeal flour
- ■ ½ tsp salt
- ■ 4 tbsp (60ml) fresh mixed herbs, finely chopped
- ■ 1 tbsp (15ml) olive oil

GLAZE

- ■ a little beaten egg
- ■ 1–2 tsp (5–10ml) sesame seeds

Illustrated above

For special occasions or just for a change, try baking bread in a clean, dry, earthenware flower pot to make a pyramid-shaped loaf. This high-fibre, herb recipe can be adapted to include any herbs you like.

PREPARATION TIME: 2 hours

COOKING TIME: 40–45 mins

MAKES: approx one 1½lb (750g) loaf

METHOD

1 Cream the yeast and sugar and mix with 3–4 tbsp (45–60ml) of the warm water.

2 Mix the wholemeal flour with the salt in a large bowl. Add the herbs and mix well.

3 Pour on the yeast mixture, adding the oil and the remaining water, and work to a dough. Knead well. Transfer to a clean bowl, cover with oiled clingfilm or a damp cloth and leave for 30–45 minutes or until well risen.

4 Knead again briefly. Shape into a round and place in a well-greased flower pot. Leave to prove for about 30–45 minutes or until well risen.

5 Brush with beaten egg and sprinkle with sesame seeds. Bake in a preheated oven at Gas Mark 7, 425°F, 220°C for 40–45 minutes. Turn out on to a wire rack. Serve hot or cold.

FROM LEFT: Onion bread; Cheese and herb bread

■ ONION BREAD ■

INGREDIENTS

- 2 tsp (10ml) olive oil
- 1 medium onion, peeled and very finely chopped
- 1–2 cloves garlic, crushed
- 2 tsp (10ml) creamed horseradish
- 1lb (500g) wholemeal dough (see p.118)

GLAZE
- a little beaten egg
- 1 tbsp (15ml) poppy seeds

Illustrated above

Onion bread is moist and fairly rich, so there is no need to add butter.

PREPARATION TIME: 30 mins (plus 50 mins for making the basic dough)
COOKING TIME: 25–30 mins
MAKES: approx one 1lb (500g) loaf

METHOD

1 Heat the oil in a pan and gently fry the onion until softened but not coloured. Add the garlic and fry for 2–3 minutes. Mix in the horseradish and leave the mixture to cool.
2 Roll out the dough into a short thick oblong. Using your fingertips, make several indentations. Spoon over the onion mixture. Roll the dough around the filling and knead briefly. Shape into a loaf and place in a well-greased 1lb (500g) loaf tin. Cover and leave to prove for 20 minutes then glaze.
3 Bake in a preheated oven at Gas Mark 7, 425°F, 220°C for 25–30 minutes. Cool on a wire rack.

■ CHEESE AND HERB BREAD ■

INGREDIENTS

- 1lb (500g) wholemeal dough (see p.118)
- 2oz (50g) Cheddar cheese, grated
- 1 tsp (5ml) dried thyme (or 1 tsp/5ml garlic powder)

Illustrated above

Cheese and herbs are among the most popular accompaniments to bread. Here, they are mixed with the dough to make a deliciously flavoured loaf, ideal with soups and starters.

PREPARATION TIME: 30 mins (plus 50 mins for making the basic dough)
COOKING TIME: 25–30 mins
MAKES: approx one 1lb (500g) loaf

METHOD

1 Roll out the dough into a short thick oblong. Using your fingertips, make several indentations.
2 Scatter over the cheese and herbs and roll up the dough, then knead briefly.
3 Shape into a loaf and place in a well-greased 1lb (500g) loaf tin. Make a long slit down the dough from one end of the loaf to the other. Cover the dough with a damp cloth. Leave to prove for at least 20 minutes.
4 Bake in a preheated oven at Gas Mark 7, 425°F, 220°C for 25–30 minutes. Cool on a wire rack.

■ CROISSANTS ■

INGREDIENTS

■ ½oz (15g) fresh yeast
■ 1 tsp (5ml) soft brown sugar
■ 8 tbsp (120ml) warm milk
■ 8oz (250g) wholemeal flour
■ pinch sea salt
■ 1 egg, beaten
■ 1 tbsp (15ml) sunflower oil
■ 2–3oz (50–75g) butter or margarine, chilled

GLAZE
■ a little beaten egg

Illustrated right

If you reduce the amount of fat in the traditional croissant version, the result is less rich but just as delicious. It is important to chill the dough well before adding the margarine so that the croissants have that distinctive flaky texture when cooked. If you want fresh croissants in the morning, leave the dough in the fridge overnight, then complete the rolling out before breakfast.

PREPARATION TIME: 2½ hours
COOKING TIME: 15–20 mins
MAKES: approx 8–10 croissants

METHOD

1 Cream the yeast and sugar together with the warm milk.
2 Mix the flour with the salt in a bowl. Pour over the yeast mixture, then add the egg, reserving a little for the glaze, and the sunflower oil.
3 Work to a soft dough and knead well, adding a little extra flour or water if necessary. Transfer to a greased bowl and cover with oiled clingfilm. Leave in the fridge for 30 minutes.
4 Roll out to a small oblong and lightly mark the dough in three. Add half the butter or margarine, by folding and rolling out (see right). Then turn the dough and repeat the rolling and folding, before wrapping loosely in oiled clingfilm and placing in the fridge for 30 minutes.
5 Repeat using the remaining margarine, then chill again. Roll and fold once more. Roll out the dough into a large circle and divide into 8–10 wedge shapes (see right).
6 Roll up each wedge loosely, beginning at the widest part. Shape into a crescent. Place on a greased baking sheet. Cover and leave to prove for 15–20 minutes. Brush with the remaining egg.
7 Bake in a preheated oven at Gas Mark 7, 425°F, 220°C for 15–20 minutes. Cool on a wire rack. Serve warm.

■ MAKING CROISSANTS ■

*T*he sophisticated elegance of the Continentals is epitomized by the "petit-déjeuner francais" – the French breakfast of warm croissants and freshly ground coffee. These are a delicious wholefood variation made with unrefined flour.

1 Roll out the dough into an oblong. Mark into 3 sections and place half the butter on the top two-thirds.

2 Fold the bottom third up and the top third down. Quarter turn, roll out and fold again. Leave to chill, then repeat.

3 Roll the chilled dough into a large circle and divide into wedges. Roll up each one, starting at the widest part.

BRIOCHE ■

This delicious and attractive loaf works extremely well with wholemeal flour provided that the mixture is beaten thoroughly at each stage, especially during the last 10 minutes. If it is not beaten sufficiently the loaf will be very heavy.

PREPARATION TIME: 4¾ hours
COOKING TIME: 30–35 mins
MAKES: one 2–2½ pint (1.2–1.5 litre) brioche

INGREDIENTS

- ½oz (15g) fresh yeast
- 1 tsp (5ml) clear honey
- 6 tbsp (100ml) milk, warmed
- 10oz (300g) plain wholemeal flour, sifted
- 4oz (125g) margarine or butter, melted
- 3 eggs
- good pinch salt

GLAZE (optional)
- a little beaten egg

Illustrated right

METHOD

1 Dissolve the yeast and honey in the milk. Add 3oz (75g) of the flour and beat until very well blended.
2 Beat in the margarine or butter and beat again until smooth.
3 Beat in the eggs, one at a time, reserving a little of the egg for the glaze.
4 Add the remaining flour and salt. Beat for at least 10 minutes.
5 Transfer to a large, greased bowl. Cover with oiled clingfilm or a damp cloth and leave in the fridge to rise for at least 4 hours, or overnight.
6 Knead again briefly. Reserve 2–3oz (50–75g) dough for the top. Put the rest of the dough into a large brioche mould.
7 Make a small indentation in the top, then mould the remaining dough into a small round and place on top. Cover with oiled clingfilm or a damp cloth and leave to prove for 20 minutes, or until well risen. Brush with beaten egg.
8 Bake in a preheated oven at Gas Mark 7, 425°F, 220°C for 30–35 minutes. Cool on a wire rack. Serve warm.

Brioche

Bagels (see p.126)

Croissants

■ BAGELS ■

INGREDIENTS

- ½oz (15g) fresh yeast
- 1 tsp (5ml) clear honey
- ¼ pint (150ml) warm water
- 12oz (375g) plain wholemeal flour
- 1 tsp (5ml) salt
- 1 tbsp (15ml) sunflower oil
- 1 egg, beaten

GLAZE

- a little beaten egg
- ½ small onion, peeled and finely chopped (or 1–2 tsp/ 5–10ml sea salt)

Illustrated on page 125

These are traditional Jewish rolls – unusual in that they are boiled before baking. The dough is enriched with egg. Wholemeal flour makes a heavier but more nutritious version than those made with white flour.

PREPARATION TIME: 1¼ hours
COOKING TIME: 20–25 mins
MAKES: 10–12 bagels

METHOD

1 Cream the yeast and honey with the warm water in a large bowl.
2 Add 3oz (75g) of the wholemeal flour. Stir in well, cover with oiled clingfilm or a damp cloth and leave for 20 minutes for the yeast to activate.
3 Sift the remaining flour and salt. Mix into the batter adding the oil and egg. Knead well. Transfer to a clean bowl. Cover with oiled clingfilm or a damp cloth and leave to rise for 20–30 minutes or until well risen.
4 Divide the dough into 10–12 pieces and roll each piece into a long thin rope, then form into a circle, pressing the ends firmly together. Cover with oiled clingfilm or a damp cloth and leave to prove for 15–20 minutes.
5 Bring a large pan of water to the boil. Boil the bagels, 4–6 at a time, for 7–10 minutes. They will sink at first, then rise to the top and expand. Remove from the water and drain.
6 Place on a greased baking sheet. Brush with beaten egg and sprinkle with onion or sea salt. Bake in a preheated oven at Gas Mark 6, 400°F, 200°C for 20–25 minutes until golden brown. Serve warm or heat through, if kept until the next day.

Poori

■ POORI ■

INGREDIENTS

- 4oz (125g) finely milled plain wholemeal flour, such as pastry or chapatti flour
- 2oz (50g) semolina
- ¼ tsp salt
- groundnut or sunflower oil for deep frying

Illustrated above

Pooris, classic Indian breads, are made from a plain dough that puffs up when cooked. They make a light, crisp accompaniment to dips and curries. Although deep-fried they need not be greasy.

PREPARATION TIME: 1¼ hours
COOKING TIME: 2–5 mins
MAKES: approx 9 pooris

METHOD

1 Mix the flour with the semolina and salt in a bowl. Add enough water to make a soft pliable dough. Knead well. Transfer to a clean bowl. Cover with oiled clingfilm or a damp cloth and leave for 1 hour.
2 Divide the dough into 9 pieces. Roll out each one evenly into a small round about ¼ inch (5mm) thick (see right). Keep the dough you are not working with under a damp cloth.
3 Heat the oil in a large pan. Test that it is hot enough by adding a small piece of dough; it should sizzle immediately and rise.
4 Slide one of the pooris into the oil, taking care it does not fold in half. Keep submerged until it puffs up, then cook for 30 seconds (see right).
5 Remove with a slotted spoon and drain on absorbent kitchen paper. Keep warm while cooking the remaining pooris. Serve immediately.

■ MAKING POORI ■

*T*hroughout the world people have developed breads to complement their national culinary specialities. It is worth the extra effort of making a traditional Indian bread like poori to accompany a curry dish. Make sure the oil is very hot before adding the poori dough or it will not cook properly.

1 Roll out the dough into small rounds about ¼ inch (5mm) thick, keeping the dough you are not using covered.

2 Heat the oil until very hot. Submerge the poori until it puffs up, then cook for 30 seconds.

3 Remove the cooked poori with a slotted spoon and drain on absorbent kitchen paper.

INGREDIENTS

■ 8oz (250g) plain wholemeal flour
■ ¼ tsp salt
■ ½ tsp bicarbonate of soda
■ 8fl oz (250ml) natural yogurt

Illustrated on page 128

INGREDIENTS

■ ¼oz (7g) yeast
■ ¼ pint (150ml) skimmed milk, warmed
■ 8oz (250g) plain wholemeal flour
■ ½ tsp salt
■ 2oz (50g) solid vegetable fat, melted
■ 1 tbsp (15ml) natural yogurt

GLAZE
■ a little milk

Illustrated on page 128

■ NAAN ■

Naan are classic Indian flat breads, made from a yogurt dough and dry-fried.
PREPARATION TIME: 1¼ hours
COOKING TIME: 6–10 mins
MAKES: approx 9 naan

METHOD

1 Sift the flour, salt and soda in a bowl. Add the yogurt slowly and mix to a soft dough. Knead well and leave covered with oiled clingfilm or a damp cloth for 1 hour.
2 Divide the dough into 9 pieces. Roll each one into a round about ¼ inch (5mm) thick. Heat a thick cast-iron skillet or griddle iron until quite hot. Place each naan in the pan, then keeping the heat even, fry for 3–5 minutes on either side.
3 The naan should puff up slightly and have a mottled look on the surface. For serving, keep warm wrapped in a clean cloth.

■ PRETZELS ■

Originally from Alsace and Germany, pretzels are a brittle, salted, biscuit-type roll in the form of a loose knot.
PREPARATION TIME: 1 hour
COOKING TIME: 10–15 mins
MAKES: approx 16 pretzels

METHOD

1 Mix the yeast and warm milk together.
2 Mix the flour with the salt in a bowl. Pour over the yeast mixture, melted fat and yogurt. Work to a smooth dough and knead well, adding a little more flour if necessary. Transfer to a clean bowl. Cover with oiled clingfilm or a damp cloth and leave for 20–30 minutes or until well risen.
3 Knead again briefly. Divide the dough into 16 pieces. Roll out each piece into a long thin rope. Bend the loose ends over to form a 'B' shape. Place on a greased baking sheet. Cover and leave to prove for 10–15 minutes. Bake in a preheated oven at Gas Mark 7, 425°F, 220°C for 10–15 minutes. Brush with milk while still warm.

■ PITTA BREAD ■

INGREDIENTS

- ■ 1oz (25g) fresh yeast
- ■ 2 tsp (10ml) soft brown sugar
- ■ ¾ pint (450ml) warm water
- ■ 1½lb (750g) plain wholemeal flour
- ■ 1 tsp (5ml) salt
- ■ 1 tbsp (15ml) sunflower oil

Illustrated left

These pocket breads, which originated in the Middle East, can now be bought in wholemeal varieties in the supermarket, or you can make your own. They make excellent sandwich cases for snacks and picnics.

PREPARATION TIME: 1¼ hours
COOKING TIME: 3–5 mins per batch
MAKES: approx 18 pitta breads

METHOD

1 Cream the yeast and sugar together and mix in ¼ pint (150ml) of the warm water.
2 Mix the flour with the salt in a bowl. Pour over the yeast mixture and add the remaining water and the oil.
3 Work to a smooth dough and knead well. Transfer to a clean bowl. Cover with oiled clingfilm or a damp cloth and leave for 30–40 minutes or until well risen.
4 Knead again briefly. Cut the dough into 3oz (75g) pieces and shape into rolls. Roll out into oval shapes. Place on a floured baking sheet. Cover with oiled clingfilm or a damp cloth and leave to prove for 15–20 minutes.
5 Pre-heat a heavy skillet or baking sheet. Place the breads on the hot sheet, fitting on 2 or 3 at a time.
6 Bake in the lower part of a preheated oven at Gas Mark 7, 425°F, 220°C for 3–5 minutes.
7 Wrap in a damp tea towel to cool – this gives them their leathery look. Split and fill as required.

CLOCKWISE FROM TOP: Pretzels (see p.127); Pitta bread; Naan (see p.127)

FROM LEFT: Corn bread ; Oat and buttermilk soda bread

■ CORN BREAD ■

INGREDIENTS

■ 3oz (75g) cornmeal
■ 3oz (75g) plain wholemeal flour
■ 1½ tsp (7.5ml) baking powder
■ ½ tsp salt
■ 1 egg
■ ¼ pint (150ml) skimmed milk
■ 1 tbsp (15ml) clear honey
■ 1 tbsp (15ml) olive oil

Illustrated above

The combination of yellow cornmeal and wholemeal flour makes a light golden bun which is quick and easy to make.

PREPARATION TIME: 10 mins
COOKING TIME: 15–20 mins
MAKES: one 6 inch (15cm) round loaf or nine buns

METHOD

1 Mix the cornmeal, flour, baking powder and salt in a bowl.
2 Beat the egg thoroughly. Add the milk, honey and oil and beat again until well mixed.
3 Add the liquid mixture to the flour to make a soft batter. Add a little more flour if it seems too runny. Spoon into a lightly greased 6 inch (15cm) sandwich tin or 9 bun tins.
4 Bake in a preheated oven at Gas Mark 6, 400°F, 200°C for 15–20 minutes or until risen, golden brown and firm to the touch. Cool on a wire rack.

OAT AND BUTTERMILK ■ SODA BREAD ■

INGREDIENTS

■ 12oz (375g) plain wholemeal flour
■ 4oz (125g) porridge oats
■ 1 tsp (5ml) salt
■ 1 tsp (5ml) bicarbonate of soda
■ ½ pint (300ml) buttermilk or ordinary milk
■ 1 tbsp (15ml) clear honey

Illustrated above

This unyeasted loaf is easy to make and the oats give it a lovely creamy flavour. If you want to make a smaller quantity, simply divide the ingredients in half. Ordinary milk could be used instead of buttermilk.

PREPARATION TIME: 10 mins
COOKING TIME: 45–55 mins
MAKES: approx one 1½lb (750g) loaf

METHOD

1 Mix the flour with the oats, salt and soda in a bowl.
2 Add the buttermilk and honey and mix quickly to a soft dough.
3 Shape into a cob and make a cross on the top. Place on a floured baking sheet.
4 Bake in a preheated oven at Gas Mark 7, 425°F, 220°C for 20 minutes, then reduce the oven temperature to Gas Mark 6, 400°F, 200°C for 25–35 minutes. Cool slightly on a wire rack and eat while still warm.

SCONES, MUFFINS ▌ AND CAKES ▌

CLOCKWISE FROM TOP LEFT: Ginger bran muffins (see p.132); Popovers (see p.132); Cheese and parsnip muffins (see p.132); Spicy cheese popovers (see p.133)

■ GINGER BRAN MUFFINS ■

INGREDIENTS

- 6oz (175g) plain wholemeal flour
- 2 tsp (10ml) baking powder
- ½ tsp salt
- 1 tsp (5ml) ground ginger
- 1 tsp (5ml) ground mixed spice
- 1oz (25g) bran
- 2 eggs
- 2oz (50g) soft brown sugar
- ¼ pint (150ml) skimmed milk

Illustrated on page 131

Quickly prepared, sweet muffins are ideal for breakfast or tea, making a healthy, low-fat alternative to cake.

PREPARATION TIME: 15 mins
COOKING TIME: 20–25 mins
MAKES: approx 9 muffins

METHOD

1 Sift the flour with the baking powder, salt, ginger and mixed spice in a bowl. Stir in the bran.
2 Beat the eggs thoroughly, then beat in the sugar and milk. Pour the mixture over the dry ingredients. Mix thoroughly.
3 Spoon the mixture into 9 well-greased, deep muffin tins.
4 Bake in a preheated oven at Gas Mark 6, 400°F, 200°C for 20–25 minutes. Eat while still warm.

CHEESE AND ■ PARSNIP MUFFINS ■

INGREDIENTS

- 12oz (375g) parsnips
- 1 tbsp (15ml) olive oil
- 1 medium onion, peeled and finely chopped
- 2oz (50g) unbleached plain white flour or cornmeal
- 2oz (50g) plain wholemeal flour
- 1½ tsp (7.5ml) baking powder
- ½ tsp salt
- 1 egg
- 2 tbsp (30ml) milk
- 1–2oz (25–50g) Cheddar cheese, grated

Illustrated on page 131

Savoury muffins can be served with soups or salads to make a quick nutritious meal.

PREPARATION TIME: 30 mins
COOKING TIME: 20–25 mins
MAKES: approx 9 muffins

METHOD

1 Scrub or peel the parsnips and dice finely. Steam or boil for about 15–20 minutes until soft. Mash well. Meanwhile, heat the oil in a pan and gently fry the onion until soft.
2 Mix the white flour or cornmeal with the wholemeal flour, baking powder and salt. In a separate bowl, beat the egg thoroughly, then whisk in the milk.
3 Mix the liquid with the dry ingredients, adding the parsnip purée, fried onion and Cheddar cheese. Mix well, then spoon the mixture into 9 well-greased, deep muffin tins.
4 Bake in a preheated oven at Gas Mark 6, 400°F, 200°C for 20–25 minutes. Serve warm.

FROM LEFT: Hot cross buns; Mixed seed muffins (see p.134)

■ POPOVERS ■

INGREDIENTS

- 5oz (150g) plain wholemeal flour
- pinch salt
- 1 tbsp (15ml) sunflower oil
- 8fl oz (250ml) skimmed milk
- 3 eggs

Illustrated on page 131

These light, low-fat buns should be eaten while still warm. Serve this plain version with sweet or savoury spreads.

PREPARATION TIME: 10 mins
COOKING TIME: 30–40 mins
MAKES: 9–12 popovers

METHOD

1 Mix the flour with the salt in a bowl.
2 Beat the oil, milk and eggs together, then pour over the flour.
3 Beat very well for at least 3 minutes. The consistency should be like double cream; add a little more flour if necessary. Pour into 9–12 well-greased, deep bun tins.
4 Bake in a preheated oven at Gas Mark 5, 375°F, 190°C for 30–40 minutes until well risen and shrunk from the edges of the tins. Serve warm.

HOT CROSS BUNS

INGREDIENTS

- ½oz (15g) fresh yeast
- ¼ pint (150ml) milk, warmed
- 1oz (25g) soft brown sugar
- 2 tbsp (30ml) sunflower oil
- 1 egg
- 8oz (250g) plain wholemeal flour
- pinch salt
- 1 tsp (5ml) mixed ground spice
- 1 tsp (5ml) ground cinnamon
- ½ tsp ground allspice
- 2oz (50g) currants
- 1 tsp (5ml) grated lemon rind

FOR THE CROSS

- 2oz (50g) ground almonds
- 1 egg yolk
- 1 tsp (5ml) lemon juice
- 1–2 tsp (5–10ml) clear honey

GLAZE

- a little beaten egg
- 1 tsp (5ml) clear honey

Illustrated left

Hot cross buns with a good spicy taste are delicious, so this recipe has been adapted to use more spices. The almond paste for the crosses needs to be quite well sweetened or it becomes dry once cooked – otherwise leave the buns plain.

PREPARATION TIME: 1½ hours
COOKING TIME: 15–20 mins
MAKES: 6–8 buns

METHOD

1 Cream the yeast, milk and sugar together. Mix in the oil and egg and beat well.
2 Sift the flour with the salt and spices into a bowl. Pour over the yeast mixture. Work to a dough and knead well. Transfer to a greased bowl. Cover with oiled clingfilm or a damp cloth and leave to rise for 30 minutes, or until well-risen.
3 Knead again briefly, then work in the currants and lemon rind.
4 Divide the dough into 6–8 pieces and shape into buns. Mark each one with a deep cross, using a knife. Place on a greased baking sheet. Cover with oiled clingfilm or a damp cloth and leave to prove for 20 minutes, or until well risen.
5 For the almond crosses, mix all the ingredients together to form a stiff but pliable paste. Press out and cut into strips. Form two strips into a cross shape, pressing them firmly together where they cross.
6 Place a cross on top of each bun. Brush all over with beaten egg.
7 Bake in a preheated oven at Gas Mark 7, 425°F, 220°C for 15–20 minutes. Brush with honey while still warm.

SPICY CHEESE POPOVERS

INGREDIENTS

- 5oz (150g) plain wholemeal flour
- pinch salt
- 1 tbsp (15ml) sunflower oil
- 8fl oz (250ml) skimmed milk
- 3 eggs
- 4oz (125g) natural cottage cheese
- pinch chilli powder
- black pepper

Illustrated on page 131

A spicy version of plain popovers.
PREPARATION TIME: 10 mins
COOKING TIME: 30–40 mins
MAKES: 9–12 popovers

METHOD

1 Mix the flour with the salt in a bowl.
2 Beat the remaining ingredients together, then pour over the flour.
3 Beat very well for at least 3 minutes. The consistency should be like double cream; add a little more flour if necessary. Pour into 9–12 well-greased deep bun tins.
4 Bake in a preheated oven at Gas Mark 5, 375°F, 190°C for 30–40 minutes until well risen and shrunk from the edges of the tins. Serve warm.

■ MIXED SEED MUFFINS ■

Quick to prepare, these muffins can be served with sweet or savoury toppings. The seeds and malted wheat in the granary® flour not only provide excellent texture, but also valuable vitamins and minerals.

PREPARATION TIME: 10 mins
COOKING TIME: 20–25 mins
MAKES: approx 9 muffins

INGREDIENTS

- 3oz (75g) granary® flour
- 4oz (125g) plain wholemeal flour
- 1½ tsp (7.5ml) baking powder
- ½ tsp salt
- 1oz (25g) sunflower seeds
- 1oz (25g) sesame seeds
- 2 eggs
- ¼ pint (150ml) milk
- 1 tbsp (15ml) malt extract
- 1½oz (40g) soft brown sugar

Illustrated on page 133

METHOD

1 Mix the flours with the baking powder, salt and seeds. Beat the eggs. Whisk in the milk, malt extract and sugar.
2 Pour this liquid over the dry ingredients and stir thoroughly. The mixture should have the consistency of a thick batter; add a little more milk if it seems dry.
3 Spoon the batter into 9 well-greased, deep muffin tins and bake in a preheated oven at Gas Mark 6, 400°F, 200°C for 20–25 minutes. Cool on a wire rack. Serve warm.

Chelsea buns

■ CHELSEA BUNS ■

A slightly plainer version of the classic recipe but just as popular. I find that soaking the dried fruit makes it sweeter and helps to keep the buns moist.

PREPARATION TIME: 1½ hours
COOKING TIME: 15–20 mins
MAKES: 10–12 buns

INGREDIENTS

- 2oz (50g) currants
- ¼ pint (150ml) apple juice
- 1 tsp (5ml) grated orange rind
- ½oz (15g) fresh yeast
- 2½fl oz (65ml) warm milk
- 1oz (25g) butter or margarine
- 1 egg
- 2–3oz (50–75g) soft brown sugar
- 10oz (300g) plain wholemeal flour
- pinch salt

GLAZE

- a little beaten egg (optional)

Illustrated left

METHOD

1 Stew the currants in the apple juice with the orange rind for 20 minutes, then leave to cool.
2 Mix the yeast and warm milk together.
3 Melt half the butter or margarine. Add to the yeast mixture with the egg and 1oz (25g) sugar. Beat well, adding 3oz (75g) of the flour. Leave in a warm place for 15 minutes for the batter to ferment.
4 Beat in the remaining flour and the salt. Draw to a dough. Knead. Transfer to a greased bowl. Cover with oiled clingfilm or a damp cloth and leave for 30 minutes, or until well risen. Roll out to a large rectangle. Spread over the remaining margarine. Drain the currants, mix with remaining sugar and sprinkle over.
5 Roll up the dough from the long side and cut into 1½ inch (4cm) sections. Place on a greased baking sheet (see right). Cover and leave to prove for 20 minutes, or until well risen. Brush well with beaten egg. Bake in a preheated oven at Gas Mark 6, 400°F, 200°C for 15–20 minutes.

MAKING
■ CHELSEA BUNS ■

*C*helsea buns originate from Chelsea, London, where they were first made in the 18th century. The traditional recipe was made from a rich dough of butter, eggs, sugar, milk and white flour. This wholemeal version is equally delicious.

1 Roll out the dough to a large rectangle. Spread with half the butter or margarine and sprinkle with currants.

2 Roll up the dough from the long side to form a sausage shape.

3 Cut the "sausage" into 1½ inch (4cm) buns. Place sideways on a baking sheet, leave to prove until well risen, glaze, then bake.

Date slice

■ DATE SLICE ■

INGREDIENTS

■ 3oz (75g) dried dates
■ 3oz (75g) sultanas or raisins
■ 2oz (50g) dried apricots or dried bananas
■ 2oz (50g) hazelnuts
■ 1–2 tsp (5–10ml) honey
■ 2–3 tbsp (30–45ml) orange juice
■ 1½oz (40g) ground almonds
■ 1½oz (40g) porridge oats

Illustrated above

High in fibre and rich in vitamins and minerals, these slices are also naturally sweet and make a rich, filling snack. They will be at their best served in small slices, straight from the fridge.

PREPARATION TIME: 15 mins
SERVES: 4

METHOD

1 In a food processor, grind the dates, sultanas or raisins and apricots or bananas with the hazelnuts until fairly smooth.
2 Add the honey, orange juice and ground almonds. Grind again until the mixture begins to bind together. Add enough oats to give the mixture a firm texture.
3 Press the mixture into a 7 inch (18cm) square tin, lined with greaseproof paper and chill.
4 Turn out and cut into thin fingers.

Barm brack

■ BARM BRACK ■

INGREDIENTS

■ 1lb (500g) currants
■ ½ pint (300ml) apple juice
■ 1oz (25g) soft brown sugar
■ 9oz (275g) plain wholemeal flour
■ 1 tsp (5ml) baking powder
■ pinch salt
■ 1 tsp (5ml) ground allspice
■ 2 eggs, lightly beaten
■ 2 tsp (10ml) grated orange rind

Illustrated above

This richly fruited teabread originated in Ireland. Traditionally, dried fruit is soaked in tea to moisten the texture, but fruit juice produces a sweeter result.

PREPARATION TIME: 15 mins (plus overnight soaking)

COOKING TIME: 50–60 mins

MAKES: approx one 1½lb (750g) loaf

METHOD

1 Soak the currants in the apple juice and sugar overnight, or simmer very gently in the sweetened apple juice for 15 minutes, then leave to cool.
2 Mix the flour with the baking powder, salt and allspice in a bowl. Mix in the currants, eggs and orange rind. Stir well.
3 Put into a small, greased cake tin or a large loaf tin.
4 Bake in a preheated oven for 50–60 minutes at Gas Mark 5, 375°F, 190°C. Cool on a wire rack. Serve cold.

■ ORANGE SAVARIN ■

INGREDIENTS

■ 6oz (175g) plain wholemeal flour
■ pinch of salt
■ 3fl oz (75ml) milk
■ ½oz (15g) fresh yeast
■ 2 tsp (10ml) soft brown sugar
■ 2oz (50g) butter or margarine
■ 2 eggs

SYRUP

■ ¼ pint (150ml) orange juice
■ 2oz (50g) soft brown sugar
■ 1–2 tbsp (15–30ml) Cointreau

GARNISH

■ 3–4 oranges, peeled and segmented
■ 1–2 tbsp (15–30ml) Cointreau or Benedictine
■ 1–2 tbsp (15–30ml) soft brown sugar

Illustrated right

Savarin is traditionally light and airy and heavily soaked in sugar syrup, but this healthy version is just as delicious. Wholemeal flour gives a slightly more substantial base and the fruit juice marinade is very refreshing. Make sure the sponge is well soaked and serve with fresh fruit. A savarin mould is a ring mould with a rounded top.

PREPARATION TIME: 1½ hours (plus 2–3 hours soaking time)

COOKING TIME: 20 mins

MAKES: One 1½ pint (1 litre) savarin

METHOD

1 Mix the flour and salt in a bowl.
2 Heat the milk, stir into the yeast and sugar and whisk well. Stir into the flour.
3 Melt the butter or margarine and beat into the flour mixture with the eggs. Cover with oiled clingfilm or a damp cloth and leave to rise for 30 minutes, or until well risen. Beat well again.
4 Pour into a lightly buttered 1½ pint (1 litre) savarin mould. Cover with oiled clingfilm or a damp cloth and leave to prove for 30 minutes in a warm place.
5 Bake in a preheated oven at Gas Mark 6, 400°F, 200°C for 20 minutes.
6 Turn out and cool slightly on a wire rack. Replace in the mould and prick the surface with a fine skewer.
7 For the syrup, heat the orange juice, sugar and Cointreau and simmer for 4–5 minutes. Pour over the cooked savarin. Leave to soak for 2–3 hours.
8 For the garnish, marinate the orange segments in the liqueur and sugar and chill.
9 Turn out the savarin and decorate with the marinated oranges and serve with yogurt or cream.

Orange savarin

Filled tea ring

■ FILLED TEA RING ■

INGREDIENTS

■ 1oz (25g) fresh yeast
■ 1 tbsp (15ml) clear honey
■ 8fl oz (250ml) warm milk
■ 1lb (500g) plain wholemeal flour
■ ½ tsp salt
■ 2oz (50g) ground almonds
■ 1oz (25g) butter
■ 1 egg, beaten

FILLING

■ 4oz (125g) poppy seeds
■ 4oz (125g) ground hazelnuts
■ 2 tbsp (30ml) rum
■ 1 tsp (5ml) lemon rind

GLAZE (optional)

■ a little beaten egg
■ 1 tbsp (15ml) poppy seeds or finely chopped nuts

Illustrated left

A basic sweet dough can be filled with all kinds of ingredients and, when rolled up, makes a most impressive tea ring. This filling is a traditional Jewish poppy seed and nut filling, flavoured with rum, which has a good dark colour.

PREPARATION TIME: 2 hours
COOKING TIME: 30–35 mins
MAKES: 16 pieces

METHOD

1 Cream the yeast with the honey, milk and 4oz (250g) flour. Beat until smooth. Cover with oiled clingfilm or a damp cloth and leave for 30 minutes, or until frothy.
2 In a separate bowl mix the remaining flour, salt and almonds. Rub in the butter. Pour on the yeast mixture and add the beaten egg, then knead well, adding a little more milk if necessary, to make a soft dough. Put in a clean bowl, cover with oiled clingfilm or a damp cloth and leave for 45–60 minutes, or until well risen.
3 Meanwhile, make the filling by mixing all the ingredients together thoroughly.
4 Knead the dough again briefly. Roll out to a large oblong. Spread over the filling and loosely roll up the dough into a sausage shape. Shape into a ring, pinching the edges together. Make 16 cuts round the dough so that the ring can rise evenly. Place on a greased baking sheet.
5 Cover with oiled clingfilm or a damp cloth and leave to prove for 20 minutes. Brush with beaten egg and sprinkle with poppy seeds or nut pieces.
6 Bake in a preheated oven at Gas Mark 7, 425°F, 220°C for 30–35 minutes. Cool on a wire rack.

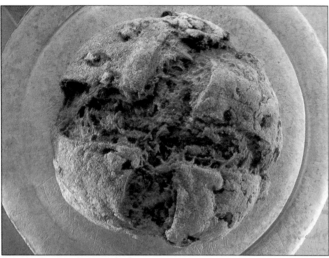

Spiced sultana and nutmeg loaf

SPICED SULTANA AND NUTMEG LOAF ■

INGREDIENTS

- ¾oz (20g) fresh yeast
- ¼ pint (150ml) warm water
- 1oz (25g) soft brown sugar
- 12oz (375g) plain wholemeal flour
- 4oz (125g) unbleached white flour
- ½ tsp salt
- ½ tsp grated nutmeg
- 2 tsp (10ml) grated orange rind
- 1 tsp (5ml) grated lemon rind
- 4oz (125g) sultanas
- 4oz (125g) skimmed milk soft cheese or quark

Illustrated above

In this fruit bread recipe, orange and lemon complement the bread perfectly.

PREPARATION TIME: 1¾ hours
COOKING TIME: 30–35 mins
MAKES: approx one 1¾lb (875g) loaf

METHOD

1 Cream the yeast, warm water and sugar together. Add 3oz (75g) of the wholemeal flour and put in a warm place for 15 minutes to ferment. Mix the remaining wholemeal flour with the white flour, salt, nutmeg and rinds in a bowl. Add the yeast mixture, sultanas and soft cheese. Work to a soft dough and knead well, adding more warm water if necessary. Transfer to a clean bowl. Cover with oiled clingfilm or a damp cloth and leave to prove for 40–45 minutes, or until well risen.

2 Knead again briefly. Shape into a large cob. Make two cuts in the top. Place on a greased baking sheet. Cover with oiled clingfilm or a damp cloth and leave to prove for 20 minutes, or until well risen. Bake in a preheated oven at Gas Mark 7, 425°F, 220°C for 30–35 minutes. Cool on a wire rack.

■ SIX-POINT STAR BRAID ■

INGREDIENTS

- ½oz (15g) fresh yeast
- ¼ pint (150ml) warm milk
- 2 tbsp (30ml) molasses
- 14oz (425g) plain wholemeal flour
- ½ tsp salt
- 1 tsp (5ml) ground mixed spice
- ¼ tsp ground cloves
- 2 eggs
- 2 tbsp (30ml) sunflower oil
- 2oz (50g) currants (optional)
- 2 tsp (10ml) grated orange rind
- 1 tsp (5ml) grated lemon rind

FILLING

- 3oz (75g) ground almonds
- 2 tsp (10ml) lemon juice
- 1–2 tbsp (15–30ml) clear honey
- 1 egg yolk

GLAZE

- a little beaten egg white
- 2 tsp (10ml) clear honey

Illustrated right

This is an attractive, sweet centrepiece for any festive occasion and the plaiting is not complicated once you have grasped the basic idea. Marzipan filling adds extra protein and richness. You could serve this bread plain, or with a low-sugar fruit spread.

PREPARATION TIME: 1¾ hours
COOKING TIME: 30–35 mins
MAKES: approx one 1¼lb (625g) loaf

METHOD

1 Cream the yeast, warm milk and molasses together.

2 Sift the flour with the salt and spices into a bowl. Add the yeast mixture, eggs, oil, currants and fruit rinds.

3 Work to a dough and knead well, adding more flour or liquid if necessary. Transfer to a clean greased bowl. Cover with oiled clingfilm or a damp cloth, and leave to rise for 30–40 minutes.

4 For the filling, combine all the ingredients into a smooth ball.

5 Knead the dough again briefly. Divide into twelve pieces. Roll each piece into a rope and place in three groups of four.

6 Plait each group of four strands until halfway up the ropes (see right), then fold the unplaited ends back so there are two on either side of the plait.

7 Place the three semi-plaited pieces on a greased baking sheet as if they are the spokes of a wheel (see right). Each plaited piece will now be separated by four loose ends. These loose ends can then be plaited together so that the whole piece has six plaited points.

8 Place the almond filling firmly in the centre of the star. Cover with oiled clingfilm and leave to prove for 20–30 minutes in a warm place.

9 Brush with beaten egg white. Place a bowl of steaming water in the bottom of the oven and bake the loaf in a preheated oven at Gas Mark 7, 425°F, 220°C for 10 minutes. Reduce the oven temperature to Gas Mark 6, 400°F, 200°C and bake for a further 20–25 minutes.

10 Cool on a wire rack. While still warm, brush with honey.

MAKING A SIX-POINT STAR BRAID

*T*his decorative loaf can seem dauntingly complicated, but the only problem is plaiting with four
strands instead of the more usual three. Once you get
the hang of this, it is not difficult at all and the delicious
flavour deserves to be complemented with an attractive
appearance.

1 *Take the right rope over the middle two ropes, then the left rope over the single strand into the middle.*

2 *Take the two right-hand ropes across into the centre. Repeat the process from the left, until half plaited.*

3 *Arrange the dough so that each plaited group is divided by a group of ends. Plait these into 3 more "points".*

FROM TOP: Six-point star braid; Muesli loaf (see p.140)

■ MUESLI LOAF ■

INGREDIENTS

■ ½oz (15g) fresh
yeast
■ 1 tsp (5ml) clear
honey
■ ½ pint (300ml)
warm water
■ 12oz (375g) plain
wholemeal flour
■ 4oz (125g) muesli
(unsweetened)
■ 2 tbsp (30ml)
skimmed milk
powder
■ ½ tsp salt

GLAZE

■ a little beaten egg
■ 1–2 tbsp (15–30ml)
poppy seeds
Illustrated on page 139

This unusual loaf uses the natural
sweetness of honey. Good for a tea bread as
a healthy change from cake or as a natural
breakfast bread.

PREPARATION TIME: 1¾ hours
COOKING TIME: 30–35 mins
MAKES: approx one 1¾lb (750g) loaf

METHOD

1 Cream the yeast, honey and warm water
together.
2 Mix the wholemeal flour with the
muesli, skimmed milk powder and salt in a
bowl. Add the yeast mixture.
3 Work to a smooth dough and knead well
adding more flour or liquid if necessary.
Transfer to a clean bowl. Cover with oiled
clingfilm or a damp cloth and leave to rise
for 30–40 minutes.
4 Knead again briefly. Shape into a loaf.
Put into a greased 2lb (1kg) loaf tin.
5 Cover with oiled clingfilm and leave to
prove for 30–40 minutes. Brush with
beaten egg and decorate with poppy seeds.
6 Bake in a preheated oven at Gas Mark 7,
425°F, 220°C for 30–35 minutes. Cool.

Spiced saffron braid

■ SPICED SAFFRON BRAID ■

INGREDIENTS

■ ½ tsp saffron
■ ¼ pint (150ml)
boiling water
■ ½oz (15g) fresh
yeast
■ 1 tbsp (15ml) clear
honey
■ 14oz (425g) plain
wholemeal flour
■ ½ tsp salt
■ ½ tsp ground
cardamom
■ ½ tsp ground
cloves
■ 1 egg
■ grated rind and
juice of ½ orange
■ 1–2 tbsp (15–30ml)
milk (optional)

FILLING

■ 4oz (125g) dried
vine fruits
■ juice of ½ orange
■ 2oz (50g) flaked
almonds
■ 2oz (50g) soft
brown sugar

GLAZE

■ a little beaten egg
■ 1–2 tsp (5–10ml)
clear honey
■ 1–2 tbsp (15–30ml)
flaked almonds
Illustrated left

This attractive braided loaf is surprisingly
easy to make. Saffron adds an appealing
golden glow to the bread.

PREPARATION TIME: 1¾ hours
COOKING TIME: 25–30 mins
MAKES: approx one 1¼lb (625g) loaf

METHOD

1 Infuse the saffron in the water. Allow
the water to cool to blood heat, then cream
in the yeast and honey. Mix the flour, salt
and spices in a bowl. Pour over the yeast
liquid and add the egg, orange rind and
juice, and milk (if using). Work to a smooth
dough and knead, adding extra flour or
liquid if necessary. Transfer to a greased
bowl. Cover with oiled clingfilm and
leave to rise for 30–40 minutes, or until
well-risen.
2 For the filling, soak the vine fruits in
orange juice for at least 30 minutes, then
mix in the flaked almonds.
3 Knead the dough then roll out to a flat
oblong. Place the filling down the centre,
sprinkle evenly with sugar, then mark out
diagonal cuts, about 1 inch (2.5cm) wide,
on either side. Weave these neatly over the
filling, sealing with beaten egg.
4 Place the braid on a greased baking
sheet and let it prove for 20–30 minutes, or
until well-risen. Brush with beaten egg and
bake in a preheated oven at Gas Mark 7,
425°F, 220°C for 25–30 minutes. Cool on a
wire rack. Top with honey and almonds
while still warm.

▮ COOKS' NOTES ▮

CONVERSIONS AND SIZES

▮ For all recipes quantities are given in both imperial and metric measures. Follow either set but not a combination of both because they are not interchangeable. Standard spoon measures are used in all recipes and all spoon measures are level.

▮ 1 tablespoon = one 15ml spoon

▮ All eggs used in the recipes are size 3 unless otherwise stated.

▮ All fruit and vegetables are assumed to be medium-sized unless otherwise stated.

TIPS FOR PREPARATION AND COOKING

▮ To speed up preparation time, canned pulses can be used instead of dried pulses. Pulses roughly double in weight when cooked so, for example, if a recipe specifies 8oz (250g) dried pulses, you will need a 15oz (432g) can. Canned pulses do not need to be cooked, but the can should always be drained before use. Where a recipe uses the "cooking stock" from the beans, for example in soups and casseroles, make up the required liquid using water and a vegetable stock cube.

▮ If fresh herbs are unobtainable, use dried herbs instead, but halve the quantity stated as their flavour is stronger.

▮ Use freshly ground pepper where pepper is specified.

▮ To save time and effort, use "no-pre-cook" lasagne and cannelloni, instead of standard dried pasta, as it is much easier to work with.

▮ Prepare fresh chillies under running water and take care not to rub your eyes while doing so. Wash your hands thoroughly afterwards.

▮ Ovens should be pre-heated to the specified temperature.

▌ INDEX ▌

■ ACKNOWLEDGMENTS ■

EDITOR Lesley Gowers
DESIGNER Phil Kay
MANAGING EDITOR Jemima Dunne
MANAGING ART EDITOR Derek Coombes
PRODUCTION Jeanette Graham
PHOTOGRAPHY Martin Brigdale
    Alan Duns
    Graeme Harris
    Graham Miller
    Ian O'Leary
    Charlie Stebbings
    Clive Streeter
ILLUSTRATIONS Lorraine Harrison
TYPESETTING Goodfellow and Egan Limited
REPRODUCTION Colourscan, Singapore

Dorling Kindersley would like to thank:
Candida Ross-Macdonald and Roger Tritton
for editorial assistance and Jean Gay for the
proofreading and index.